GON
WAY
TRUTH

HISTORIC GRAVES OF GALWAY

RÓNÁN GEAROID Ó DOMHNAILL

Dedicated to my grandmother,
Agnes Boyle 1915–2015
Folk healer and beloved by many

First published 2016

The History Press Ireland
50 City Quay
Dublin 2
Ireland
www.thehistorypress.ie

The History Press Ireland is a member of Publishing Ireland, the Irish book publishers' association.

British Library Cataloguing in Publication Data.
A catalogue record for this book is available from the British Library.

ISBN 978 1 84588 904 3

Typesetting and origination by The History Press

Printed and bound by TJ International Ltd.

CONTENTS

Acknowledgements

I am thankful to many people for this project. I thank Ronan Colgan, Beth Amphlett and the staff of The History Press Ireland, Gary Branigan for his encouragement and tips, Eamonn Boyle for revealing so much local lore and bringing me to many of the sites, Joe Glynn, Pat and Fergus Hessian, the staff of the National Library and Tuam Library, Eva Brackmann, Manus Ó Domhnaill, Órla Ní Dhomhnaill, Michael McDonagh, Joe Hegarty, Ray Sully from New Cemetery, Richard Forde, Cormac Ó Comhraí, Séighean Ó Draoi, Andy and Sady Fuery, Eileen Morris, Hubert Birmingham, Rebecca Hayes of the Freemason Archives, Matt Doyle of the National Graves Association, Mayor Catherine Carlton of Menlo Park, California, Director of Pavee Point Martin Collins, Sister Mary M. Mount Carmel, Loughrea, John and Eimer Mahony, Ruairí Ó hAodha of the Old Tuam Society.

About the Author

Rónán Gearóid Ó Domhnaill was born in Dublin and raised in Galway city where his father's family lived for several generations. He was educated at St Patrick's National School, Coláiste Iognáid and UCG (NUIG), where he studied Irish, German, philosophy and history. He lived abroad for several years in Dresden and Vienna. He completed his masters in German in 2005 before returning to Ireland to work as a teacher. His previous books include *Alte Irische Mythen und Legenden* (2002), a collection of Irish legends written in German and launched at the Frankfurt Book Fair, *Fadó Tales of Lesser Known Irish History* (Troubador, 2013) followed by a sequel *Fadó Fadó More Tales of Lesser Known Irish History* (Matador, 2015). He lives in Dublin and blogs at www.ronangearoid.blogspot.ie.

Introduction

History is not about dates, places and wars.
It is about the people who fill the spaces between them.

JODI PICOULT

Gone the Way of Truth is a journey through Galway's rich and varied past illustrated by graves of note. The title itself may appear somewhat unusual and is a translation from the Irish *imithe ar shlí na* fírinne, a euphemism for death, apt given Galway's close connection with the Irish language and culture. Graveyards are for many associated with morbidity but they are also fascinating places to explore and form an under-explored portal to a bygone era. The gravestones themselves are monuments to people who once walked the streets and bohreens of Galway. They formed the fabric of what it meant to be a Galwegian. Galway city has experienced many changes, going from remote English outpost in an Irish-speaking sea to bilingual capital of Ireland. The county is also home to a considerable amount of little-known mausolea belonging to the Anglo-Irish gentry, who became invisible after 1922 and saw their contribution to Galway life airbrushed out of history. This book will examine Galwegians of many different hues: they will be presented to the reader for what they were – part of the Galway story, and judgements of their character will be left to the reader.

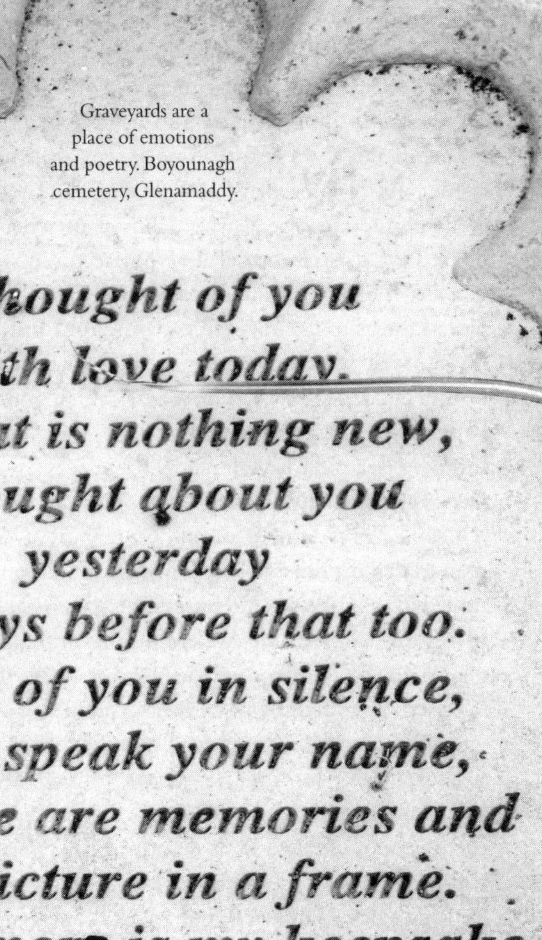

Graveyards are a place of emotions and poetry. Boyounagh cemetery, Glenamaddy.

Gravestones are at times unwelcome reminders of a darker, more cruel past, of things that went on that should not have happened. Letterfrack and the Magdalene Laundry are two examples of this and, unpleasant as they might be, it would be disingenuous of me to gloss over them and leave them out of Galway's story. Galwegians serving with the RIC have also been deleted from history. Their graves are not always easy to find as they were not stationed in their home county. Thus, many RIC fatalities in the county are not covered because the deceased were buried elsewhere and, in some cases, denied a Christian burial. The police force was poorly regarded, but, after nearly a hundred years of independence, enough time has passed for us to examine all aspects of our history. They form part of the story of Galway. There should be no illusions about the War of Independence: it was a dirty war, which got dirtier as time went by with atrocities committed by both sides. For those interested in further research, I have included their service numbers after their names as I have with British Army personnel.

I came across some books on Galway graveyards, but what struck me was that they merely listed the inscriptions on the graves and gave no details about who the buried were or what kind of history the graveyards had. At times we are reliant on folk memory, and as old people die so do their memories. It is important that they be recorded. If we know something of the background to these stone memorials we will appreciate them more. I travelled the city and county extensively searching for forgotten graves. In many ways, getting out and about and seeing what is still left was the most pleasant part of compiling this book. Many graves described have never been highlighted before and some suffer from neglect. A crude cross in the cathedral's car park where Galway Gaol once stood reveals little of who is buried there. In Bohermore Cemetery, in an unmarked and forgotten grave, are the mortal remains of Arthur Colohan, the man who wrote the famous song, 'Galway Bay'. A graveyard in Clifden contains the grave of the last secretary-general of the League of Nations, Seán Lester, one of the few people in power to stand up to Hitler during the era of appeasement. In Clonfert we can find the grave of St Brendan, a saint well known beyond Ireland and in Indreabhán the graves of

Dr Noel Browne and Renvyle Oliver St John Gogarty, while Rahoon Cemetery inspired James Joyce.

Sadly, the lack of piety which has crept into our society has led to an increase in vandalism and desecration of old graves. It is my intention to ensure that the mortal remains that occupy these graves are not forgotten: the greatest respect we can afford the dead is to have their names spoken once more and cherish their graves. To me it seems like a contradiction that we can honour someone yet neglect and forget about their final resting place. Grave inscriptions fade. As the inscriptions fade away, so too does our memory of those who once were part of Galway. By highlighting these graves I have tried to create a greater awareness for our culture and hopefully encourage their preservation. The stories within these pages also make Galway a more interesting place. At this stage I must apologise to Galwegians for the graves I have neglected to mention, but I hope the stories that I have included will rekindle interest in deceased Galwegians who have been long forgotten. All photos are my own unless otherwise stated.

Rónán Gearóid Ó Domhnaill, Dublin 2016

Gravestones, such as this one at Adergoole near Milltown, can be centuries old.

1

Types of Graves

Viva enim mortuorum *in memoria vivorum* *est posita.*	The life of the dead is retained in the memory of the living.

CICERO

Graves have taken many different forms over the ages and there is great variety present in County Galway. There are of course graves dating as far back as the Bronze Age (2000 BC – 400 BC) in Galway, but these places of burial have already been covered extensively in other books. The reader will notice that at times I use the word 'graveyard' and at other times 'cemetery'. Graveyards tend to be older and have a church attached, while cemeteries, more common from the late nineteenth century onwards, as populations grew and people wanted burials outside the city centre for health and safety reasons, do not. Christians introduced the practice of burying the dead with the head facing west and the feet east. Early medieval burials tended to be in shallow graves with a burial shroud being used rather than a coffin. The most ancient Christian burial ground in Galway city is at Roscam on the shores of the bay. One of the oldest early Christian graves in the county is a seventh-century slab found at Ard Oileán or High Island near Inisboffin.

Recumbent grave slabs, long and narrow slabs placed on the ground, usually decorated with a cross, were used between the twelfth and seventeenth centuries. An example is the 'Crusader's' grave at the church of St Nicholas in Galway city, and others can be found at Roscam and Drumacoo. Burial within a church was usual

One of the heraldic gravestones on display at Ross Errilly. It reads 'Pray for the sol [*sic*] of Andrew (?) Fitz Peter and his wife Ann Bodkin [who died in] 1720.' The Fitz Peters lived in Cummer, Corofin.

until the eighteenth century, though this was the preserve of the clergy and the wealthy. Wall panels became fashionable from the late seventeenth century and examples can be seen at Ross Errily and St Nicholas' church. They often have the heraldic coat of arms like the one at Claregalway friary. Headstones started appearing around the late seventeenth century as the middle class began to have their names inscribed on their graves.

Many such headstones have long sunken into the ground or are tilted, a sign of an old graveyard. Headstones tend to be limestone or granite, the latter being more resistant to the dissolving effect of acid in rainwater. Marble was introduced in the nineteenth century, though it was too expensive to be used extensively. It is interesting to observe that inscriptions on gravestones that are centuries-old can be very legible, while inscriptions on gravestones only a few decades-old might no longer be legible. I asked a stonemason, Séighean Ó Draoi, why this is so. Until the twentieth century, stonemasons hand-carved the letters and the quality of work was far superior to what is produced today. These days, inscriptions tend to be sandblasted and the lettering quite shallow. The stone used today tends to be polished, imported granite and the paint comes away more quickly. When the paint comes away and the polish fades, the inscription becomes harder to read. On the older graves, the V-cut lettering is deeper and sharper and, even without paint, the inscription is quite legible. The V-cut lettering in limestone and slate generally lasts better than in granite. Protection from the elements also plays a part. Records are kept of burials within the last 100 years or so but no record is kept of what inscription was on the individual grave. Sadly, once they become weathered beyond recognition, they are lost and gone forever. Grave rubbings sometimes work. A rag and water also do the trick. Tin foil will also show the imprint of the headstone. The inscriptions of lichen-infested gravestones are impossible to decipher without the use of photogrammetry, whereby a tridimensional image can be created allowing you to see what lies beneath the lichens.

Grave inscriptions vary in style. In the nineteenth century, spelling mistakes were not uncommon with the words often being engraved as they were pronounced. It mattered little as most people were illiterate anyway. Sometimes missing letters would be subsequently engraved between the letters. While today the sans serif lettering is the most common form, more ornate lettering such as copperplate script was commonplace in the eighteenth century, as in the mort house at Roscahill. On pre-nineteenth century gravestones the lettering was sometimes raised, like on the Bodkin grave at Fort Hill. A common feature on nineteenth-century graves was the use of lead lettering, which, in the absence of high-resolution paint, highlighted the engraving and was very durable, a characteristic that was required if the inscription was to withstand the Galway weather. Lead lettering usually came in one of two forms: beaten and hammered smooth or raised in relief, and it is often associated with prosperity. A good example of this is the forgotten grave of Alice Burns or Sebastian M. Nolan in New Cemetery. Right up until the nineteenth century, grave inscriptions remained the preserve of the wealthy, and the gravestones of the poor tended to be low, uncut fieldstones without any engraving. The use of wooden crosses may also account for many nineteenth-century graves being unmarked today; their lifespan, in a damp climate like Galway's, would not exceed fifty years. Simple stone crosses, such as the ones I encountered at Adergoole, near Milltown, are akin to those at Skellig Michael and could be up to 1,000 years old.

Effigies of knights on tombs are a rarity in Galway. Indeed, the only example I know of is at Glinsk. There are, however, several types of tombs that can be found in Galway. Wall tombs, adjoined to a wall, sometimes with a canopy, are the oldest and date from around the fifteenth century. A chest tomb, a tomb supported by four panels, generally dates from the nineteenth century. Under these chest tombs is usually a barrel-shaped vault, lined with red bricks, which is often a few yards deep. Table tombs also became fashionable in the nineteenth century. As the name suggests, table tombs look like a table with four legs, with a space underneath the grave slab. Obelisks were considered tasteful monuments that symbolised past greatness and required little space. They were also cheaper than a sculpted figure. Variations of these include urns on pedestals and truncated pillars. In New Cemetery, the grave of Alexander Moon, to the left of the main gate, is a good example of this.

Vaults are sometimes found under churches. An example of this is the Blake vault at Bushypark. Sometimes a mort house was constructed over

A wall tomb with canopy, Kiltartan.

the vault or crypt like at Roscahill. The obelisk was influenced by the discoveries made in Egypt and began to appear in graveyards from the mid-nineteenth century. The county has a number of mausolea, many of which are covered within these pages. A mausoleum is an external free-standing building with a doorway, constructed as a monument enclosing the interment space or burial chamber of a deceased person or people. Mausolea were designed to stand out and, needless to say, were the preserve of the wealthy, mostly the ruling Anglo-Irish gentry.

Some belong to the descendants of the Tribes of Galway who, after the seventeenth century, were intermittently Catholic or Protestant. Lead coffins are usually to be found within, unless they have been removed to prevent desecration from vandals, an unfortunate malaise of our society, as respect for graves in a secular society diminishes.

A monument without any interment is referred to as a cenotaph. An example of a cenotaph is the polished granite one in the graveyard of St Nicholas' Collegiate church in the city, erected to three teenagers who lost their lives on the Corrib. These tend to be late nineteenth century or early twentieth century. There are older cenotaphs, in the form of mounds of rocks common in Galway. I came across a nice example near Headford. Inis Mór on the Aran Islands has several. Memorial plaques, especially in the Church of Ireland, became commonplace from the eighteenth century onwards.

The Celtic Revival of the late the nineteenth century saw the reintroduction of the Celtic cross, which can be seen in many different forms. Nobody knows for sure what the circle in the cross symbolises. It may be an old pagan symbol or represent the halo of Christ, or it may quite simply be a support for the cross. These crosses are still being used in many variations, though they are now subject to height restrictions.

Some nineteenth-century gravestones are encased in iron, but this is very rare. The only example I came across in the whole county was in the old graveyard in Dunmore. Crosses made of iron are also to be seen in some graveyards and tend to be of a late nineteenth-century vintage.

Yew trees are a common feature in graveyards. There are a number of reasons for choosing this tree. It was sacred among the Celts and its branches do not shed their leaves in winter, thus perhaps

Above: A chest tomb at Menlo for Ellis Donelan (d. 1899) and her husband.
Right: One of the many variations of the Celtic cross, which became popular during the Celtic revival of the late nineteenth century. This example is at Reilig na Bréanana near Maam. The Holy Trinity is symbolised by the fleur-de-lis. The harp may symbolise Irish nationalism or in the case of a broken string, the break with mortal life.

R I P
PRAY FOR

symbolising eternity. There was a more practical reason for having yew trees in graveyards – their leaves are toxic to cattle, which were notorious for trampling through graveyards. Lawn cemeteries are relatively rare in Galway. They are usually modern, flat, manicured lawns with no grave boundaries. Furbo graveyard, behind the local church, was one of the few examples I encountered.

There are a number of symbols to be found on graves. The most common is IHS meaning *Iesus Hominum Salvator* (Jesus, saviour of men). Clasped hands often symbolise a married couple who were separated by death. A lamb, symbolising innocence, is sometimes found on the gravestones of children. A weeping willow symbolises mourning and grief. A tree stump symbolises a life cut short and suddenly taken away. Ivy symbolises faithfulness, memory, and undying friendship, while a laurel stands for victory and fame. A draped or broken column represents the break in earthly life. A broken branch or drooping flower often indicates that the person died prematurely. A broken chain symbolised a loss in the family. An anchor is not necessarily connected with the sea and can symbolise hope or a safe harbour. Birds represent the soul, a dove purity, love and the Holy Spirit. A torch symbolises eternal life and, if upturned and extinguished, death.

Spelling was not always deemed important as seen on this gravestone in Ahascragh. Note also the inverted letter N.

2

THE *CILLÍN*

There's two buried 'neath the stable door
Another two near the kitchen door
Another two buried beneath the wall.

ANON, 'THE WELL BELOW THE VALLEY' ('THE MAID AND THE PALMER')

To the modern mind, the notion of burying someone outside a normal graveyard seems bizarre, but it was a practice that went on for at least 1,000 years, right until the advent of Vatican II in the mid-1960s. Until then it was believed that unbaptized children were not allowed into heaven and their burial outside the graveyard was symbolic of their status in limbo. The *cillín* is a common feature on any Ordnance Survey map, though many were never marked at all on any map despite existing in nearly every parish in the county. Some areas have more than others, and Seán Spellisy, in his book *The History of Galway* (1999), maintained that the Dunmore area, containing fifty-two, has the largest amount of these burial grounds in the county. The county is believed to 420 in total. The word *cillín* itself is the diminutive of *cill*, which comes from the Latin *cella* meaning church or monastic cell. *Cillíní* are often beside the abandoned ruins of early Christian churches. They are also referred to on maps as killenn, calthagh, caltra, children's burial ground or lisheen.

'In memory of the innocents interred elsewhere in this area', Killfhursa, Headford.

They can be hard to find as, more often than not, the cemetery is just a clump of randomly arranged upright rocks, overgrown by weeds. Some *cillíní* are in good repair and enclosed by a mound of earth or stones. Within the enclosure, which may be circular or rectangular, are at times stones in neat rows. In some rare cases, the stones are inscribed. Deirdre Crombie, who conducted a study of *cillíní* in the barony of Dunmore, wrote about one in Ballymoat where there was an inscription to both an adult and a child. It was not just unbaptised children who were interred there, but also suicide victims and even vagrants and other strangers. At Addergoole More, there are three cross-inscribed slabs within the *cillín*.

In some cases, the *cillíní* are found within a ringfort or lisheen. The ringfort, also known as a fairy fort, was linked to taboos passed down from generation to generation: this ensured both their survival and that of the *cillíní* within them. Another example of using an ancient place is close to Mam Éan, a mountain pass in the Maamturks, not far from Recess, which has been a gathering place since ancient times. Traditionally, a dead baby would be

Monument to a *cillín* at Lavally.

buried between dusk on the day it died and sunrise the next day. The father with the help of a neighbour buried them. They were not always buried in a *cillín*, but sometimes where two ditches met or under the threshold of the cottage door. It was also common to bury them on the border of two townlands, which symbolised their status in limbo. As with the Great Famine, it is only recently that an interest has been shown in them. Since this is within living memory, they represent a painful, unspoken part of life for older people with a sibling buried in one their grief could not be openly expressed, and it is only recently that the injustice has being rectified. Even up until the twentieth century there was quite a

The former site of a *cillín* at Ceathrú Rua.

A children's graveyard on the site of the old county infirmary.

high infant-mortality rate in the county. In a quiet corner of a city council car park, just off Bóthar na mBan, is a graveyard for children who died in the county infirmary and were not given a headstone. There were definitely *cillíní* within the city boundaries, but they have been erased with the passage of time. One such *cillín* was at Blackrock on the golf course. The commemorative stone reads:

> This segment of the foreshore is traditionally known as a burial place. On the early Ordnance Survey map a small rectangular enclosure is marked close to this spot and called Kilnapastia (church of the children). It was common practice in the past to choose sites such Killens for the burial of unbaptised children and strangers. The plaque has been erected by Galway Golf Club to mark the approximate location of this ancient site.

Cuireadh iad ar shlí *na mara. Táid anois* *ar shlí na fírinne.*	They were placed by the sea. Now they are gone the way of truth.

During the infamous Celtic Tiger years, many of these *cillíní* were built on. In Rahoon, there was a case of poltergeist activity in a house built on what was believed to be the site of a baby's grave.

At Ceathrú Rua's famous 'Coral' beach, An Doilín, an inscribed boulder reminds the visitor of the *cillín* that was there until the road was widened in the 1990s. It may be translated as follows:

> Children's strand, protected in the arms of Mary, may they lie before the Lord, our infants without names, and their weeping relatives, taken from us, during the famine, the local community erected this stone in 1997.

Toward the end of the 1990s, an awareness for these burial grounds came about and monuments and plaques initiated by local community groups started appearing.

3

THE GREAT FAMINE

The Great Famine was the single most tragic disaster to befall Galway within the last 200 years and Europe's greatest social disaster of the nineteenth century. Though underpopulated today, places such as Connemara were massively overpopulated in the 1840s with little food to support an ever-growing population. Though the true number will never be known, due to poor record-keeping, it is generally accepted that nationally 1 million died during the Great Famine and that Galway was one of the worst affected areas. It may seem odd therefore that, until very recently, the famine was hardly commemorated with any monuments. There are several reasons for this: one is shame. Galwegians were not proud of their abject poverty, which caused thousands of people to starve. For decades after the terrible events surrounding the famine, its memory was suppressed. 'Famine' itself may be the wrong word to use as it implies that there was no food. On the contrary, there was food, but it was not distributed and it even got exported. In Irish the famine is referred to as *An Gorta Mór*, the Great Hunger, and some people even refer to it as a holocaust. Who or what was to blame for the famine is, however, not for me to discuss here. The famine happened, but most Galwegians would not wish to see it used as a tool to generate hate. It was not isolated and there were many more famines in the hundred years prior to that. Around 250,000 people died in the famine of 1740, for example. Although it was not discussed, it had an impact in popular culture, albeit only in the twentieth century. Writer

Liam O'Flaherty addressed it in his major work *Famine* (1937), as did Walter Macken in his work *The Silent People* (1962), which takes place in the pre-famine Ireland of 1826 when acute food shortages were also common. Academically, the topic was well covered in the 1960s by Cecil Woodham Smith's *The Great Hunger: Ireland 1845–1849* and of late by local historian William Henry who wrote *Famine: Galway's Darkest Years* (2011). It also had impact in songs such as 'The Fields of Athenry', first recorded in 1979.

So where are Galway's famine graves? The answer is: everywhere. People died by the side of the road and in ditches, their mouth green from the grass they ate in a last effort to keep starvation at bay. In some areas things were so bad that cases of cannibalism were reported. The case of Honor Flaherty from Cill Ciaráin is so horrible that no one believed her. She was apparently so desperate for food that she ate part of her dead child. The dead were not afforded elaborate tombs or even a grave marker. Most were buried in communal graves such as the one at Poll na Curtha (hole of the buried) in Oughterard or under a mound like in the old graveyard at

The Celia Griffin memorial. The stones bear the names of the ships which sailed from Galway during the famine years.

Carrowbrowne. A reference in the *Tuam Herald* from 1852 describes the graveyard surrounding Temple Jarlath in the centre of the town as being overcrowded with famine victims. A field, known locally as Dr Clarke's Field in Carrowpeter, not far from the workhouse, was also used as was a famine burial site along the Ballymote Road. A plaque was erected to the latter site in 2005 and although one was erected at Dr Clarke's Field in 1947, the burial mounds marking their graves were erased when houses were built on the site.

Fort Hill and Roscam also have famine graves, though unlike other counties such as Donegal and Tipperary, which have signposts for their famine graveyards, Galway does not seem to advertise them. The famine victims were very often buried where they died and became the subject of local lore. I heard the story of An Fear Rua, the red-haired man, from Michael McDonagh. Several decades ago, farmers came across human remains in Indreabhán while clearing a field of stones. In order not to disturb the grave, stones were piled on the spot when the field was cleared. In some cases the dead were buried within the workhouse walls, like in Mountbellew. Until the mid-twentieth century, folk tales spoke of the 'hungry grass' – it was believed that whoever stepped on the spot where someone had died during the famine would feel pangs of hunger. It became a custom to always carry food when making a journey.

A popular misconception is that most famine victims died of a lack of food. In fact, many seemed to have died from diseases such as fever, dysentery, cholera, smallpox and influenza rather than from actual starvation. The worst year was 1847, known as Black '47, when nearly 2,000 died in Galway city, a significant number given that the city would have had a population of less than 15,000. The fever did not make distinctions between rich and poor. Some of the workhouse inspectors died themselves, such as Major Patrick McKie who died in 1849 aged 34 and is buried in the graveyard of St Nicholas' Collegiate church. Landlords such as Marcus Lynch of Renmore House and Thomas Martyn of Ballynahinch, the son of Humanity Dick, Lord Dunsandle, Robert Gregory, Stepney St George, all died of the fever. Twelve priests also died of the fever. One of them, 29-year-old Revd John Roche, is buried in an impressive tomb in Bushypark.

Most of the deaths occurred in the workhouse. According to historian William Henry, between 1847 and 1848 11,000 people died in County Galway workhouses. Workhouses had been set up in 1839 at Galway, Gort, Tuam, Ballinasloe, Clifden and Loughrea. They were poorly equipped to deal with the onslaught which came to their doors and were not therefore in a condition to become centres of relief. They were dirty and disorganised and some, such as the one in Clifden, closed just before the famine. The workhouse was the last resort. Families were separated, men from women and parents from children, and they could see their loved ones only once a week. Any jobs assigned were designed to punish the inmates for being poor. For those who wish to dig deeper into this, I would recommend the Irish Workhouse Centre in Portumna. When the workhouses could no longer cope, people sought refuge in Galway Gaol, but this could only house 200.

Galway city swelled with starving people, largely avoided by the citizens of Galway for fear of catching any disease, and there were many tragic cases of people dying of starvation on the streets. On the cold morning of 26 January 1848, two children were found naked and dead on High Street and another street nearby. The case of Celia Griffin is the most poignant. The Griffin family from Corindulla near Ross, on the Martin Estate at Roscahill, had walked into Galway in the hope of getting food. The Presentation Sisters took in 6-year-old Celia and tried to give her food but she was too weak and her body refused it, which resulted in her death. The location of her grave is not known. The subsequent autopsy, the report of which is engraved onto a stone at the Celia Griffin Memorial Park, opened in 2012, states that she had no food in her stomach. This is the only famine monument in the city. Its location at Grattan Road is apt. As in the case of Threadneedle Road, it is called Bóthar na Mine in Irish, the meal road, a road built as a part of famine-relief work. The park also contains the names of the ships that carried Galwegians to a new life across the Atlantic. Not all the ships which sailed the Atlantic made it safely and many were nicknamed 'coffin ships'. The Atlantic became the grave for many. One of the most famous ships, the *Brig St John*, skippered by Claddagh man Martin

The Famine Remembrance Park,
Ballinasloe.

Oliver, sank just off the coast of Cohasset, Massachusetts in October of 1849 with a loss of ninety-nine Irish, mostly from Galway.

One of the more famous victims of the famine was Dan O'Hara, immortalised in a song made famous by Delia Murphy. Having been evicted, he was forced to go to America. The ships assumed the passengers would bring their own food, so the rations they supplied amounted to a starvation diet for the duration of a voyage that could take six weeks or longer. Moreover, the passengers were not screened for diseases before boarding. Half of Dan O'Hara's family died on the journey over and the remainder had to be placed in an orphanage. He ended his days selling matches on the streets of New York and would have faded into obscurity had Delia Murphy not composed the famous song. It is not known if his children survived, but in places like Boston during the famine years, approximately 60 per cent of Irish children died before the age of 6. By 1850, the worst of the famine was over but by then Connacht had lost more than a quarter of its population.

America has several famine monuments. There are famine graves for Galwegians at places such as Deer Island near Boston, where about 1,000 Irish are buried. The largest burial ground for famine victims is at Gross Isle near Quebec, where 5,000 Irish are buried, many of them doubtlessly from Galway. A large Celtic cross was erected to their memory by the Ancient Order of Hibernians. With few exceptions, Galway's famine monuments only date from the late 1990s. The National Famine Museum at Strokestown House in County Roscommon opened in 1994 and the Famine Memorial Park Ballinasloe opened in 1997 on a site known locally as Bully's Acre.

4

FUNERAL CUSTOMS

Bíonn an bás ar aghaidh *an tseanduine agus* *ar chúl duine óig.*	Death is facing the old and behind the young.

SEANFHOCAL/PROVERB

Galwegians were deeply superstitious right up until the mid-twentieth century. It comes as no surprise, therefore, that there should be a number of *piseogs* (superstitions) surrounding death and funerals. The old Gaelic families had a banshee attached, whose wail foretold a death within the family. Belief in this persisted into the 1970s. Another form of death messenger was the *cóiste bodhar*, the silent coach, driven by a headless coachman called a *dullahan*, whose whip was a human spinal cord. The notion of a carriage arriving to take away souls is by no means limited to Ireland. One only has to think of the Emily Dickinson poem 'Because I could not stop for Death', where death arrives in a carriage. Omens of death were also present in nature. Seeing four magpies together was regarded as an omen for death, as indeed was a robin knocking on your window or entering the house. It was believed that cats could interfere with the souls of the dead and they were not let into a wake house. If a cat did jump over the corpse, it would be killed the next day. I heard of an unusual custom from my Dunmore relatives, whereby the coffin would be taken outside the house and placed on two chairs, and one chair would be kicked away. In the nineteenth century, beds tended to have several pillows as people preferred to sleep in an elevated position. Only the dead lay flat and it was feared that to sleep flat would mean that one would not arise. When someone died, their body was washed by the women of the household about three hours later. In some places there was a table used specially for the corpse, the so-called wake table. I came across an example of this in Glenveagh Castle, Donegal. In other cases the corpse was laid out on a bed in white sheets and dressed in a woollen habit, brown for men and blue for women. The curtains of the wake house were drawn but the window of the room where the corpse lay was left open so the spirit of the deceased could exit. Unlike today, when the body is left overnight in the church, the deceased in the wake house was not left alone until burial. Pennies were often placed over the eyes. The mirrors in the wake house were turned around or covered, lest the soul become trapped inside the mirror. Clocks were stopped at the time of death as many would ask what time it was when the death occurred. Games were played at the wakes and these varied depending on the locality. They were a way of making the time pass as the mourners would wake the body all night, and this was not easy after a hard physical day's work. No wake was complete without clay pipes, which were used until the 1950s. Everyone present was expected to take a puff, the smoke of which was believed would keep away evil spirits. The clay pipes were often left on the grave and there is a photo of this at Salruck graveyard, near Leenane, in the National Library, taken by R.J. Welch on a visit to Maam in 1897. The corpse was sometimes kept for up to four days in the house. In order to reduce the smell, snuff was used.

The longer the corpse was kept out of the grave the better, otherwise the resurrection men, as corpse robbers were known, were likely to steal the body from the grave. Medical science paid handsomely for a fresh corpse in the first half of the nineteenth century. The only legitimate source of corpses, those of executed criminals, could not supply the demand and there was a thriving business in illegally procured bodies. Irish corpses were even exported to Britain. It was

One of two mortsafes in Ahascragh, the only ones left in the county.

A broken log on a grave often denotes a life cut short

not a crime to steal a corpse, but it was to steal the clothes or anything on the corpse. The resurrection men were often tipped off by gravediggers or were gravediggers themselves. The rich had mortsafes built over the grave, while the poor could only stand watch over the graves of their loved ones. The only known examples of mortsafes left in the county are in the old cemetery in Ahascragh. The coffin always exited the house feet-first. Otherwise the spirit of the deceased might try to get back into the house. In the nineteenth century, the coffin was often taken directly from the wake house to the graveyard. Sometimes, a coffin made of straw was used. In the medieval period, coffins were not really used and the body was wrapped in a shroud. Tradition demanded that the funeral procession take the longest way to the graveyard, lest the deceased think you were trying to get rid of them too soon. Businesses along the route closed and the curtains of private houses would be drawn. An unusual custom – at least, unusual by our standards – was the age-old practice of drinking the blood of a loved one. English observers confused it with cannibalism. Reference is made to this in the most famous Irish lament, *Caoineadh Airt Uí Laoghaire*, composed in the eighteenth century, in which Eibhlín drinks her dead husband's blood. Paddy Doherty, an Irish traveller and winner of *Big Brother*, also drank the blood of his dead son as a mark of respect, though the travellers I spoke to had never heard of this custom.

Graves were dug by neighbours, and this was viewed as a great honour. They were never dug after nightfall or on a Monday. While it was usual to greet men at work with the words '*Bail ó Dhia ar an obair*' or 'God bless the work', those digging a grave were greeted with 'The Lord have mercy on the souls of the dead'. The coffin was often carried the entire distance from the church or wake house to the grave at shoulder level. The pallbearers were replaced every now and then or took a rest by placing the coffin on a mound of stones or a gap in the wall. Keening, from the Irish *caoineadh*, was synonymous with the West of Ireland. The word *ochón* was often heard in Irish laments, akin to 'woe is me' in English. The keen was sometimes sung by relatives, and especially by the older women. Keening would not commence until the body had been prepared, lest it attract evil spirits. Its purpose, like firing a volley of shots over the grave, was to scare away evil spirits. The lead keener would recite a lament, and all the women of the house would join in. Nobody knows how old the keen was but it doubtlessly stemmed from pagan times. It disturbed the Anglo-Norman families of Galway to the extent that the Mayor of Galway, Marcus Ffrench Fitz John tried, albeit unsuccessfully, to have it outlawed in 1604. Despite Church opposition, it survived until the twentieth century. John Millington Synge, who spent time among the people of Inis Mór, depicted a group of women who keen the death of their loved ones lost at sea in his play *Riders to the Sea* (1904).

It is still usual for people to bless themselves when passing a funeral and for children not to play on the street where the deceased lived. To disrespect a funeral cortège brings bad luck, and when the Mayo football team did so in the 1950s, the priest cursed them saying that while the members of the team lived, Mayo would not win the All-Ireland again. Three of them still survive and the curse seems to prevail. It was also considered unlucky to fall in a graveyard or to remove anything. Even today we can leave mementoes on our graves and we take for granted that they will not be stolen. A common enough toast, especially among the Irish abroad, was '*Bás in Éirinn*' – 'to die in Ireland', the eternal wish of many of migrants to have their mortal remains interred in the old country.

5

Galway City

Táim sínte ar do thuama
agus gheobhair ann de shíor mé.
Dá mbeadh barra do dhá
láimh agam,
ní scarfainn leat choíche.
A phlúirín is an tsearc sé ann
domsa luí leat.
Mar tá boladh fuar na cré uait,
dath na gréine is na gaoithe.

Táim sínte ar do Thuama

I am stretched on your grave
And I'll lie there forever.
If your hands were in mine
I'd be sure they could not sever
My apple tree, my brightness.
It's time we were together
For I smell of the earth
And am worn by
the weather.

I am stretched on Your Grave

ANON, EIGHTEENTH CENTURY

NEW CEMETERY

> Personally, I have no bone to pick with graveyards, I take the air there willingly, perhaps more willingly than elsewhere, when take the air I must. My sandwich, my banana, taste sweeter when I'm sitting on a tomb.
>
> SAMUEL BECKETT

Directions: Leave Eyre Square and drive up the hill towards Bohermore. The cemetery is on the right before a small roundabout across from a petrol station. Parking is available.

Also known as Bohermore Cemetery and to a lesser extent St Mary's Cemetery, New Cemetery opened its gates in 1880 and was designed according to the Victorian fashion of having a graveyard away from the church, hence the name cemetery. As the city expanded, more spacious burial places were required. A quick trawl through the Internet gave the names of three famous burials: those of Lady Gregory, Lord Haw-Haw and Pádraic Ó Conaire; but there are so many more graves of note in the cemetery, the resting places of people who formed the fabric of the city over the last 100 years, and as such the cemetery is massively under-explored. The first thing the visitor notices are two chapels – Protestant on the left and Catholic on the right, though the division of graves is no longer this strict. At the same time, we are not all equal in death and as in any cemetery there are more favourable spots to be interred in than others. To help the reader track down the graves, I have divided the cemetery into four sections, with section A being to the immediate left as you go through the gates until the road that divides it from section B. Section C will then be on the top right while section D on the immediate right as you enter.

Section A

This section contains some of the oldest graves, many of which were unknown to me prior to my research for the simple reason that they were chiefly Protestant and they did not form part of the version of Irish history I was taught.

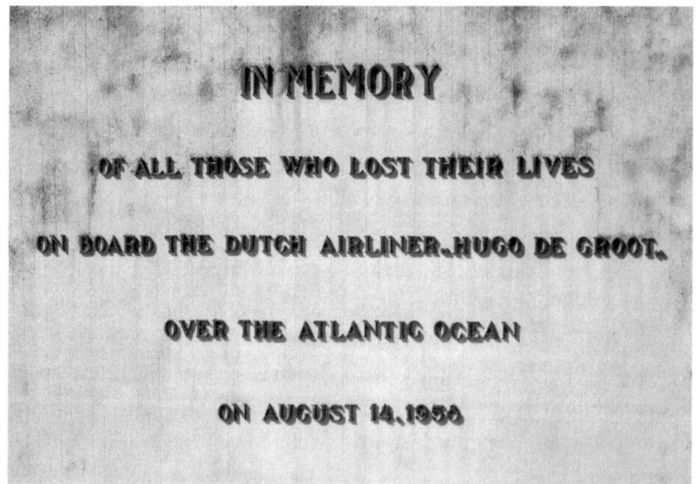

The KLM Flight 607-E disaster.

As you enter the cemetery your attention is immediately drawn to a mass grave on the left, which is for the victims of KLM Flight 607-E, also known as the *Hugo de Groot* Tragedy of 14 August 1958. The passengers were a mixture of Dutch, Israeli, American, Egyptian and Polish. The plane left Amsterdam and after having fuelled at Shannon took off at 3.05 a.m. on its transatlantic voyage. It crashed half an hour later. All of the ninety-one passengers and eight crew members died. A rescue operation was launched for potential survivors when radio contact was lost and debris was found floating in the sea 180 kilometres (110 miles) west of Shannon. The remains of thirty-four of those on board were also recovered. None of the crew members were found and the Atlantic was their final resting place. Irish and Dutch investigators were unable to establish the exact cause of the accident but it was believed it was a mechanical error. The city mobilised its voluntary emergency units to deal with the disaster and possible survivors. A French trawler, the *Jules Verne*, was the first ship to bring in bodies, watched by a large, silent crowd. The remains were brought to the Regional Hospital where Irish and Dutch doctors carried out post mortems. The only object flight investigators could work on was a wristwatch that had stopped at 5.48 a.m.

There was no evidence of death by drowning, nor were there signs of smoke damage on the deceased. A verdict of death from multiple injuries, fractures, and haemorrhages was returned at the inquest and reported to the world. Twelve of the bodies were identified and repatriated while twenty-two were buried nine days after the crash at Bohermore. As was customary, all the businesses along the cortège route closed as a mark of respect. Religious ceremonies of six different faiths were carried out at the Regional Hospital Galway, paying respect to the cultural diversity of the passengers.

The youngest casualty was eleven-month-old Bernadette de Kock van Leeuwen, buried apart from the mass grave. Children's toys adorn the solitary grey slab inscribed in Dutch. She lost her parents in the crash and her grandparents travelled from the Netherlands to attend the funeral.

Directly behind the KLM mass grave is the grave of William Joyce, better known to many as Lord Haw-Haw. He became infamous for his wartime broadcasts from Germany. He was born in Brooklyn, New York, in 1906 and the family moved to Galway soon afterwards, where he was educated by the Jesuits. He hung around with the infamous Black and Tans to whom he passed on information and in 1921, when he was 16, the IRA tried to assassinate him. The family fled to England for their safety. After studying at the University of London where he gained a first, Joyce became interested in fascism and joined Oswald Mosley's British Union of Fascists in 1932. He rose to become their director of propaganda and deputy leader until he fell out with Mosley in 1937 and moved to Germany, where he wrote *Dämmerung über England* (Twilight over England), his vision of a fascist Britain, in 1940. It was then that he commenced his infamous 'Germany calling' broadcasts. He was captured near Flensburg when, in an ill-judged show of overconfidence, he started a conversation with British soldiers, who recognised his distinctive voice. His trial began in September 1945 and when his American nationality came to light, it seemed that he would be acquitted. After all, how could he be convicted of treason when he was not a British citizen at the outbreak of hostilities? Most British also regarded him more as a figure of fun rather than as a dangerous traitor. He had lied to get a British passport,

The youngest victim of the KLM disaster.

claiming to have been born in Galway, but this lie was accepted as truth and he became the last person in Britain to be executed for treason. Albert Pierrepoint officiated. After the execution, the following statement from Joyce was posted on the gates of Wandsworth Prison and read over the airwaves:

In death as in life, I defy the Jews who caused this last war, and I defy the power of darkness which they represent. I warn the British people against the crushing imperialism of the Soviet Union. May Britain be great once again and in the hour of the greatest danger in the West may the standard be raised from the dust, crowned with the words – 'You have conquered nevertheless'. I am proud to die for my ideals and I am sorry for the sons of Britain who have died without knowing why.

The grave of William Joyce.

As with all other prisoners, Joyce was buried within the prison walls, in an unmarked grave, and no mourners were permitted. The body was dumped, in the middle of the night, on top of the remains of another man, a murderer who had been hanged five days previously. In 1976, Joyce's daughter Heather Pierce, who was 17 when he was executed, after years of trying, was finally successful in having his remains exhumed, and in the middle of the night the tarmac in Brixton Prison was dug up and the body shipped to Galway. The reburial of her father's body cost her far more than she could afford, but she had the letters he had written to his second wife, Margaret, who had died in 1972, so she gave them to a collector, in return for the price of a headstone. It is a simple grave but still tended. When I last saw the grave in October of 2015 someone had pinned a picture of Joyce and a black, white and red ribbon to the grave.

D'Arcy Wentworth Thompson came from a seafaring family and was born off the coast of Van Diemen's Land in 1829. He went on to study the Classics at Cambridge. He taught briefly in Edinburgh where one of his pupils was Robert Louis Stevenson. He was appointed professor of Greek at Queen's College Galway in 1864 and was regarded as one of the most brilliant men to ever hold a chair at the university, where he lectured for thirty-eight years. He died in 1902 and *The Galway Express* of 1 February 1902 gave a full account of the funeral. A lecture hall at the university is named after him. His son died tragically on the Corrib. On 17 August 1887, three teenaged engineering students from Queen's College Galway – John Skelton Thompson, Francis John Kinkead and Thomas Leopold Roberts – went boating on the Lough Corrib close to Headford. Thompson was the son of D'Arcy Thompson; Kinkead the son of Dr Richard Kinkead, Professor of Midwifery and Medicine; and Roberts was the son of the Revd Roberts of Oughterard. The alarm was raised when they failed to return. A search party set out, hoping that the boys had decided to camp out on one of the islands. Even if they had capsized, all three could swim and there was every chance that they had made it to an island. The body of Roberts was found near Clydagh. Thompson and Kinkead's bodies were found about 100 yards from the shore. When the boat was found it was discovered that the sail was tied down.

This probably led to the boat capsizing when the wind suddenly changed. Roberts was buried in Kilcummin Cemetery, Oughterard. Thompson and Kinkead were buried in the New Cemetery. Roberts' headstone reads:

In Memory of
Thomas Leopold Roberts
Drowned in Lough Corrib
17th August 1887 aged 18 years.
Erected in sympathy with
his parents and by his & their
Many friends of all
Creeds and Classes
Ad Mortem Fidelis

Lady Augusta Gregory was a pivotal figure in the Gaelic revival of the late nineteenth century and a founding member of the Abbey Theatre in Dublin. She was also one of William Butler Yeats' main benefactors, without whose support he would not have been able to survive as a poet. She was born in Roxborough, near Loughrea, which would later be burnt down by the IRA, in 1852 and educated privately. She married Sir William Gregory of Coole Park and the couple had an only child, Robert, born in 1881. Robert's death in the First World War inspired W.B. Yeats to write the famous poem 'An Irish Airman Foresees his Death'. Lady Gregory had met Yeats in 1895; he taught her about Irish mythology and became a frequent visitor at her home in Coole Park. At the time, Irish people learnt absolutely nothing of their ancient culture in schools. She suddenly became aware of the literary resource on her own doorstep. She wrote *Cuchulain of Muirthemne* (1902) and *Gods and Fighting Men* (1904) and was responsible for erecting a headstone over the grave of the forgotten poet Raftery.

Along with Edward Martyn and W.B. Yeats she established the Abbey Theatre in 1897 and started writing her own plays, such as *Rising of the Moon* (1907). They tended to be written in the language spoken by the local people, which she referred to as 'Kiltartanese'. Like Yeats, she believed that an art that was not rooted in the lives of the people

The grave of Lady Augusta Gregory.

The forgotten grave of Alice Burns.

was shallow. Her home and grounds at Coole Park were sold to the Forestry Commission in 1927, though she could still live out her life at the big house. She had an impressive library, which would have proven invaluable to future generations, and she stipulated in her will that it was be donated to the Irish people. Yeats is said to have sobbed like a child when he heard of her passing. Her wishes were ignored and her library was sold off separately. Although clearly an Irish patriot, who did Trojan work for the literature of this country, she did not fit into the new Ireland set-up after 1922. Indeed, as Anglo-Irish, she belonged to the 'invisible' class that were in power before 1922 but were then airbrushed out of Irish history and society. Her home was demolished soon after her death in 1932 and today only the foundation remains. The only wish respected was that she be given a simple funeral. As the *Galway Observer* of 28 May 1932 noted, 'there was nothing in the funeral or graveside service to indicate the passing for a great personage'. Her grave, a simple limestone slab inscribed with the sentence 'She shall be remembered forever', is well maintained. Her sister Arabella Persse Waithman (1850–1924) and her husband Robert Waithman (1827–1914), who lived on the site of Merlin Park Hospital, are buried either side of her.

George MacBeth (1932–1992) was a Scottish poet born in Shotts, Lanarkshire. He studied at Oxford before going to work for BBC radio. Following his divorce, he went to live at Moyne Park, Abbeyknockmoy, near Tuam. Not long after moving he contracted motor-neurone disease, of which he died in 1992. His last poem was inspired by the disease. Part of his published work included *Poems from Oby* (1982) and he received a Geoffrey Faber Memorial Prize for his work.

The grave of Alice Burns is long forgotten and the lead lettering on her headstone, highly fashionable and expensive at the time, has partially fallen away. Her funeral though was massive. The 19-year-old was shot dead in the Royal Hotel near Eyre Square on Tuesday 29 July 1884. Her murderer was Thomas Parry of Edenderry, County Offaly, with whom she had recently broken up. Burns lived in the Royal Hotel, where Supermacs in Eyre Square now stands, and was eating breakfast when Parry came in, walked up to her and, without a word, shot her. Parry then tried to shoot himself but the bullet just grazed his head. He then walked outside still carrying the gun, was overcome by passers-by and held until arrested by the RIC. He confessed to the murder immediately and expressed a wish to suffer the full rigors of the law for his crime. The funeral of Alice Burns took place on 31 July and hundreds of people from all walks of life gathered for the removal of her remains to the New Cemetery in Bohermore. Galwegians wept as the glass hearse containing her polished oak coffin, drawn by four horses draped in black, moved through the city. As this was a crime of passion, it attracted considerable media attention as far afield as New York, where it was covered by *The New York Times* which featured an article on the case the day after Thomas Parry was hanged on 20 January 1885.

An unmarked grave of note is that of Cecil Blake and his wife Eliza *née* Akerman who was pregnant at the time of her death. Both were assassinated during the Ballyturin ambush near Gort on 15 May 1921, while returning from a tennis party. Cecil Arthur Maurice Blake (1885–1921) was born in Holdenhurst, Bournemouth. After service in the First World War he became an Auxiliary in 1921. Accounts of

The resting place of Cecil Blake.

what happened vary, but it is believed that Lily refused to leave her husband's side and that the couple did not discharge their weapons in the ambush. The Blakes were interred in single graves, side by side. The RIC fired a volley of shots, while a soldier from the Connaught Rangers sounded the last post. The graves do not have a headstone and apparently one was never erected. This appears to have been a family decision. A wooden cross was erected in recent years but has since decayed and all that remains is the metal plate. Also shot in the same ambush were two officers of the 17th Lancers, Captain Cornwallis and Lieutenant Robert Bruce McCreery. They were buried in Kent and Dorset respectively. The sole survivor of the ambush was Margaret Gregory, widow of Robert Gregory and Lady Gregory's daughter-in-law. She died in 1979 in Exeter, Devonshire.

Long forgotten about is the HMS *Grappler*, a gunboat built in 1856. A gravestone commemorates William Short, the chief ERA (engine room artificer, in charge of the boiler) who died in 1891 aged 44. The ship was sold for commercial use in 1868. In 1883, a fire was discovered in her boiler while it was sailing through Seymour Narrows in British Columbia. It is believed that seventy people lost their lives when it sank, although, due to poor record-keeping, their identities could not all be established. The gravestone was erected by the officers and men of the *Grappler*.

Section B

Moving past the KLM monument, the visitor can see an impressive mausoleum, belonging to the Morris family who were Catholic. Lord Killanin, one-time attorney-general, the first Catholic one since the Battle of the Boyne, died at Spiddal in September 1901, aged 74, and was buried therein. Unlike him, his son Colonel George Morris is not actually buried here but his name is commemorated in this cemetery. He served with the Irish Guards and fell in the early stages of the First World War. The mausoleum is the final resting place of Michael Morris, 3rd Baron Killanin, MBE, TD (1914–1999). He was born in London and became a journalist. During the war he took part in the Normandy landings, which earned him the MBE. In 1945, he married Sheila Cathcart Dunlop

(1918–2007), from Oughterard, who was also awarded the MBE for her code-breaking work at Bletchley Park, a unique double for an Irish couple. Michael Morris also produced films such as *The Playboy of the Western World* (1962) and *The Rising of the Moon* (1957). He died at his home in Dublin aged 84, and following his requiem mass at Spiddal church he was brought to Bohermore.

On the right-hand side at the bottom of a hill are new headstones with old dates, the resting place of Magdalene 'penitents'. The visitor might be forgiven for thinking they have been recently restored, but the truth is that they were only recently erected. The Magdalene Laundry, run by the Sisters of Mercy, between 1922 and 1984 is an unwelcome reminder to Galway's austere and uncaring past, a past which Galwegians would rather forget. I had to ask the caretaker where these graves were. He himself had not known of their existence until their headstones were erected in 2013, after the Irish State issued a formal apology and set up a €50 million fund so their mortal remains could be finally respected. That was only after the United Nations had issued a scathing report on human rights' abuses in which

The Morris tomb.

One of the Magdalene laundry plots. The graves were unmarked until 2013. Note the absence of flowers.

the State itself was culpable. Denying them a proper headstone was the final degradation to women who had been shamefully treated in life. Even with headstones, the eight plots are easy to overlook. No reference is made to the Magdalene Laundry and they just bear the names of the deceased and their date of death, which seems to have been between 1894 and 1950. They are, however, noticeable by the complete absence of flowers or plants. How old these women were and how they died is not known, and research into this is not always facilitated by the authorities. However, many of them seem to have died around the same time. For example, five women died around 1919, a time when Spanish flu was rife. The erection of the gravestones with names inscribed was itself controversial. Not all the families wanted it known that they had disowned their own daughter and had her imprisoned. It is believed that there are around fifty women buried in these graves. Women stayed in the laundry for different amounts of time. While some were collected by their family, many were not and remained imprisoned against their will. For them, the only way out was in a coffin. The laundry closed in 1984 and the nuns sold the site in the 1990s when it was demolished to make way for houses. At the back of this housing development are four black marble headstones and in gold lettering the names of forty-one people who died between 1887 and 1954. These are the graves of women who were 'consecrated' Magdalenes, former penitents who chose to become nuns. It was a slightly less arduous existence and it meant they would be buried with dignity, unlike the those buried at Bohermore. Between the gravestones is a white statue of Mary Magdalene with a skull at her feet. A monument by Mick Wilkins, depicting a woman hanging out a sheet, was unveiled in 2009. Underneath the sculpture are the following lines from Patricia B. Brogan:

Make visible the tree,
Its branches ragged
With washed out linens
Of a bleached shroud.

Its location was controversial as it is just across from the tourist office, and its removal to a quieter location has been considered.

Galway was a 'garrison town', so it comes as no surprise that a number of British Army graves, some well-manicured and some

The graves of 'consecrated' Magdalenes watched over by the figure of St Mary Magdalene on the site of the former laundry. They were deemed worthy of a headstone when they died but why were the Magdalenes interred at Bohermore denied a headstone until 2013?

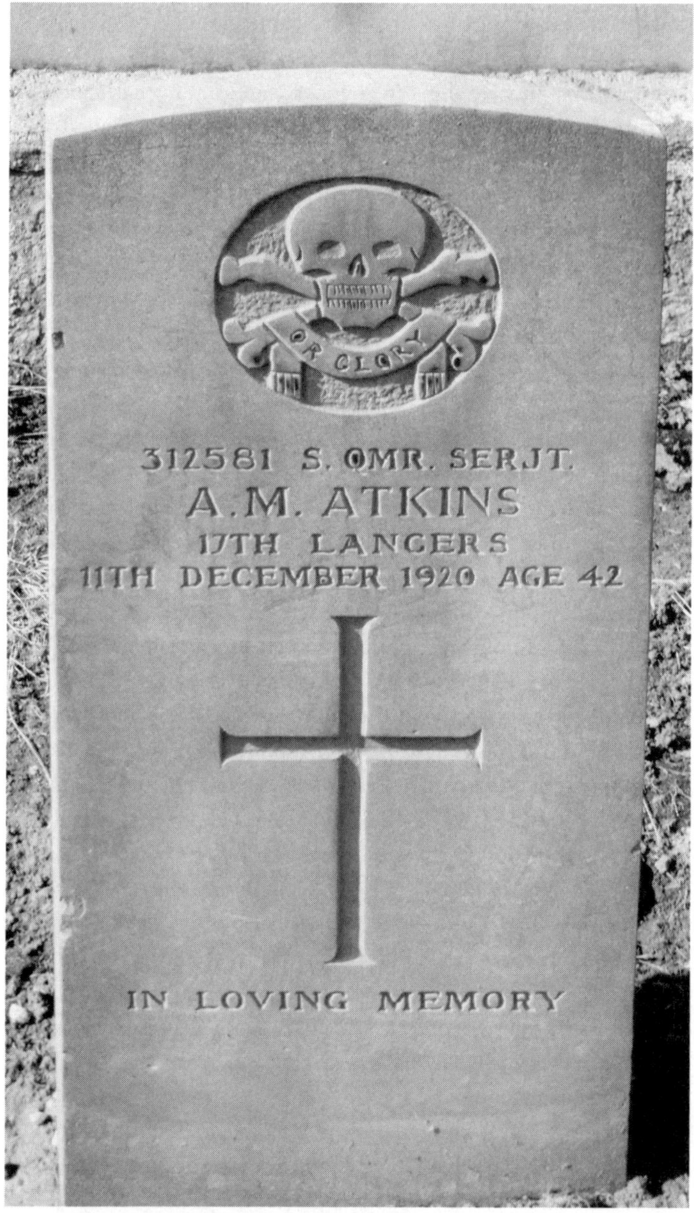

One of several British Army graves at Bohermore.

forgotten and overgrown, are in the cemetery. The 6th Dragoons were stationed on Earl's Island. They were later replaced in their constabulary duty by the 17th Lancers, a regiment that had taken part in the Charge of the Light Brigade. They often drilled their horses at low tide on the breach at Grattan Road. Although their equipment was occasionally vandalised, they do not seem to have been targeted during the War of Independence. None of the British Army dead interred at Bohermore were killed by the IRA. Arthur Michael Atkins of the 17th Lancers died by accidental drowning on the Corrib on 11 December 1920.

Sergeant William Doherty (1876–1919) of the 4th Machine Gun Corps has both a military and a civilian headstone. The cause of death does not appear to have been recorded. Equally unclear is how Private Henry Fishwick (18189), of the Welch Regiment, 21st Battalion, died on 10 October 1917. The British Legion gives his age as unknown. It is probable that he did not die in Galway at all but on the field of battle.

Three members of the 6th Dragoon Guards are buried side by side – Bishop, Thompson and Bannister. Sergeant Reginald Frank Bishop (1896–1920), was born in Farnaham, Surrey. He served on the Western Front and won the Military Medal. Bishop died of a gunshot wound to the face on 15 May 1920. He had left his gun down in the guardroom. A Private Porteous removed the magazine and, believing it to be unloaded, squeezed the trigger and shot Bishop. Private Porteous was cleared of any wrongdoing at the inquest. Private Herbert Thompson was born in 1897 in Newcastle. He was shot on 13 June 1920 by a sentry while trying to sneak back to camp when he failed to respond to the sentry's challenge. The same fate befell Private J.M. Cairns who was with Thompson. Private Alexander Frederick Bannister from Windsor, Berkshire, died by drowning when he fell out of a boat on the Corrib on 12 October 1921.

On 11 July 1921, the Truce came into effect. Even then, though, the killings did not stop. Lieutenant G.H. Souchon of the 17th Lancers was shot on 25 of September as he passed the town hall while being driven to Earl's Island. Republicans were holding a

Two fallen soldiers of the Connaught Rangers.

dance, and when British military personnel tried to get in, shots were fired and a stray round hit the unfortunate Souchon, who was to have retired a month previously, but his papers had been delayed. His body was taken to Wookham, Surrey for burial. Corporal Charles Henney, a RAF mechanic, was born in Winchcombe, Gloucestershire. He died shortly after the truce, on 18 August 1921, aged 21. His cause of death seems to be unknown. The British military departed Galway in late December of that year.

There are also a few graves from the Second World War. Private Patricia Rose Kennedy (W/280633) from Galway, the daughter of Patrick Joseph and Mary Josephine Kennedy, who served in the Auxiliary Territorial Service, died on 2 March 1945 and was buried here, as was 42-year-old Private William Skerritt (T/11057132) of the Royal Army Service Corps, who died in 1945 in Oxfordshire. Little seems to be known about the circumstance of their deaths.

Section C

An interesting RIC grave is that of Captain James Duffy, county inspector, whose date of death is given as 28 February 1921. He had fought in the First World War, serving with the Royal Munster Fusiliers, and there he was affected by gas. I had difficulty researching him as different sources contradicted each other. According to one source, he was born in Donegal and moved to Loughrea, where his father was also

Captain James Duffy of the RIC.

in the RIC and served in Callan and Oughterard, neither his home area. According to the witness statement of Tadhg Kennedy, of the Kerry IRA, Duffy was born in Tralee, had attended Blackrock College with Éamon De Valera and Paddy Cahill of the Tralee IRA and was stationed in Tralee. It would be highly unusual for a Kerry RIC man to be stationed in his home area. He decided to work with the IRA and died of his gas wounds in the Grand Hotel, Tralee and according to Kennedy was buried in Tralee. The name Duffy appears twice on the gravestone, and as local historian Cormac Ó Comhraí pointed out to me, it is spelt differently which may mean an error on the part of the stonemason or a more relaxed attitude to spelling at the time.

Walter Macken (1915–1967) was born in Galway at number 18 St Joseph's Terrace, the youngest of three children. His father fell in the First World War, leaving his mother alone to raise the family. Walter started working in the Irish language theatre An Taibhreac from the age of 17, and there he met and eloped to London with Peggy Kenny in 1937. He later returned to Ireland and worked at the Abbey, before devoting his life to writing. This was his life's ambition, and he had been writing short stories from the age of 8. In Ireland he is best known for his trilogy of Irish historical novels *Seek the Fair Land* (1959), *The Silent People* (1962) and *The Scorching Wind* (1964), set during the Cromwellian Plantation, the famine and the War of Independence respectively. Internationally, his most successful book, *Rain on the Wind* (1950), won the Literary Guild Award in America, which guaranteed sales of over 250,000 copies. His most famous children's book, *Flight of the Doves*, was made into a film in 1971 and is still shown every St Patrick's Day. His works feature ordinary Galwegians, and is based on people he met and knew. His son, Ultan, said of his father:

> His attitude to writing was based on the premise that a writer should not leave his own country, and that the life of a writer should be like that of a monk: through isolation, peace, and serenity he could be most creative. To further this, on the advice of his publisher, Macmillan, he left Dublin to find a place where he could discover this serenity.

Walter Macken.

Serenity was found at first in Oughterard and then in Menlo. His gravestone proclaims: 'People are the cornerstone of the world'.

The tallest Celtic cross in the cemetery marks the grave of Sebastian M. Nolan of Seamount Lodge, who died in 1907. His residence no longer exists but was located at Pollnarooma East, Salthill and was used as a nursing home in the twentieth century before being demolished. I found the inscription interesting: 'he bequeathed the residue of his estate as an endowment for the great charitable work of the Magdalene Asylum in Galway'. It gives the visitor an insight into how the Magdalene Laundry was viewed at the time. Major McNally of the Connaught Rangers was killed in action on 28 April 1917, while his wife Clare Eleanor was one of the victims of the *Leinster*. The *Leinster* was en route from Kingstown (now Dún Laoghaire) to Holyhead on 10 October 1918 when it was torpedoed by UB-123 close to Dublin Bay and 500 people lost their lives. Also buried at Bohermore is another victim of the sinking of the *Leinster*, Captain Ramsay Milne, of the 10th Battalion Canadian Infantry, Alberta Regiment. Originally from Montrose, Scotland, he and his wife lived in Eyre Square. He held a Military Cross and a Distinguished Service Medal. He does not have a military grave and his headstone is recognisable by a dove flying downwards. Not far away is another Connaught Rangers' grave, that of Lieutenant-Colonel Charles Smyth, who died in September 1939. The regiment became a memory after the creation of the Irish Free State in 1922, though its former members held reunions for decades afterwards. It is not just in the church of St Nicholas that memorials to this West-of-Ireland regiment are to be found, but also in the cathedral where a lesser-known stained-glass window is dedicated to them. Two other graves in the cemetery, side by side, to Privates Agnew and Roland, who fell in April of 1915, are adorned with the Connaught Ranger's crest, the crown above the heart. Other graves are at Tuam and Creagh cemeteries as well as at Kilmacdough. For readers interested in tracing family members who served in this regiment I would recommend the regiment's association based in Boyle or the National Archives in Kew in London, though many records were destroyed in the Blitz.

Section D

The Colohan family plot is most unassuming and there is no indication that it is the final resting place of Dr Arthur Colohan, the man who wrote the world-famous song 'Galway Bay'. His name is not even inscribed on the gravestone, which is bizarre given the Trojan work he did for Galway's tourism. The name of Randolph Colohan is inscribed. He died by accidental drowning on Lough Corrib in 1912. A classmate of Colohan's wrote a tribute to Randolph in the UCG College Annual of Easter 1913:

He lies within the silent tomb
So lately full of life and mirth
His dust now mingles with the earth
While nodding daises over him bloom.

Arthur Nicholas Colohan was born in Enniskillen on 12 August 1884. The family moved to Galway where they had long associations and he attended the 'Bish' and later Mungret College, Limerick as a boarder. He did an Arts degree in UCD in 1900 before going on to study Medicine, graduating as a doctor from Queen's College, Galway in 1913. He went to work at the County Infirmary (now the County Hall), before moving on to Holles Street. He joined the Royal Army Medical Corps in the First World War and was badly affected by mustard gas in India. He settled in Leicester where he spent the rest of his career as a neurological specialist. The song itself was written in 1927 and was heard by a music promoter who started playing it on the radio. It became popular later on when Bing Crosby adopted it in 1947. There are of course two songs about Galway Bay, though the older version is sometimes referred to as 'My Own Dear Galway Bay' and was written by Francis A. Fahy (1854–1935) from Kinvara on the southern shores of Galway Bay. Though buried in Putney Vale Cemetery in London, Fahy is not forgotten in his native Kinvara and is remembered with a plaque in the village. The song is rarely sung, perhaps because the hauntingly beautiful version sung by Dolores Keane cannot be matched. 'Galway Bay' is a song about the grief of exile and encapsulates the soul of Galway. It was used in the 1952 film *The Quiet Man*, but Colahan's name was not included in the film's credits. He died at his Leicester home at 9 Prebend Street off London Road on 15 September 1952 and his remains were moved to Galway for burial in the family plot.

Despite his contribution to the city's tourism, even today there is no mention of his name on the Celtic cross that marks his last resting place. Nor does there seem to be plans to honour him. There is a Doctor Colohan Road in Salthill, but the average Galwegian, who could sing a few bars of the famous song, would never have heard of Arthur Colohan. Although he is ignored in Galway, in Leicester

The forgotten grave of Arthur Colohan.

a blue plaque was mounted on the wall of his former home in 1986. The last verse of his famous song is apt here:

And if there's going to be a life hereafter
And somehow I feel sure there's going to be

I will ask my God to let me make my heaven
In that dear land across the Irish sea.

A forgotten Galway politician was my own great-grandfather, John O'Donnell (1866–1920), who was originally from Mayo. He worked as a journalist and a Nationalist politician, and after joining the United Irish League became its national secretary and enjoyed the support of William O'Brien. In the 1900 general election, O'Donnell was elected MP for South Mayo after Michael Davitt had resigned his seat in protest over the Boer War. He moved to Galway where he established the *Connaught Champion* newspaper. On 23 October 1902 he ran across the floor of Parliament and shook his fist furiously in the face of Prime Minister Arthur Balfour who had refused to discuss the Irish question. He was imprisoned for his part in the land agitation in 1905 and sentenced to two month's hard labour in Galway Gaol. He was re-elected in the January 1906 general election despite attempts by South Mayo priests to oppose him. In the January 1910 general elections O'Donnell was returned for O'Brien's newly founded All-for-Ireland League, this time through clerical support against an anti-clerical opponent. Later that year, however, he retired after receiving a lack of support and an Irish Party boycott drove his newspaper out of business in 1911. His house on Williamsgate Street, long-since demolished, was used by the Irish volunteers to drill and train. Behind his grave is that of Councillor Michael Walsh from High Street who was murdered by the Black and Tans on 19 October 1920. According to Geraldine Dillon, who gave a statement to the Bureau of Military History, he had let his farm be used as a jail for prisoners of Republican courts. His body was found on Long Walk and a plaque is embedded on the wall there to commemorate this. Only immediate relatives were allowed to follow the hearse as it moved through the city, and when more people tried to join the cortège, they were stopped from doing so by mounted soldiers of the 17th Lancers.

Close by is the grave of TD Seán Tubridy (Seán Ó Tiobraide), grandfather of the famous RTÉ presenter. He was a well-known doctor in South Connemara and, as a member of the IRA, fought in the War of Independence. He later fought with the anti-Treaty IRA and was subsequently dismissed from his job. He was a popular doctor and a considerable amount of local objection ensued, leading to his reinstatement. He played a pivotal role in fighting cholera, typhus and Spanish flu epidemics which plagued Connemara at the time, and which have largely been largely forgotten about. He represented Galway as a TD and died in 1939, aged 41.

Lieutenant Aonghus Murphy, son of General Murphy, was just 25 when he was killed in a roadside blast on 21 August 1986 in the Lebanon, where the Irish Army had been employed on peacekeeping duties since 1979. The Irish soldiers had been deliberately targeted. I remember the funeral procession as military men of different countries made their way into the cemetery on a dreary West-of-Ireland day. The grave is not marked with the Defence Forces' crest, which is unusual.

Pádraic Ó Conaire (1882–1928), also known as Sean Phádraic, was born in Galway in a building known for years as Pádraic's Place. He was

Killed in the service of peace, the grave of Aonghus Murphy.

The Pádraic Ó Conaire gravestone, unveiled at the centenary of his birth in 1982.

abandoned by his father in 1888 and orphaned in 1893. He went to live with his uncle in Ros Muc where he attended the local school and later went to Blackrock College in Dublin. He spent time in London where he wrote his famous *Deoraíocht* (Exile) in 1910, the first significant novel in modern Irish. The novel deals with an Irish emigrant in London who suffers a terrible accident and joins a travelling circus as part of their freak show. It was noted for its sympathy with the marginalised elements of our society. Like many writers, Ó Conaire was a 'heavy drinker'. He married Molly Ní Mhanais and the couple had four children. He returned to Ireland in 1914, leaving his wife and children behind, and lived a nomadic, man-of-the-road lifestyle, travelling the country with a donkey and etching a meagre existence out of his writings and work for the Gaelic League. He also wrote short stories of which *M'asal Beag Dubh* (My little Black Donkey) is the best-known. When he died at Richmond Hospital, Dublin, all he had on him was an apple and his pipe. A statue was unveiled to him by Taoiseach Éamon de Valera in Eyre Square and became a much-loved symbol of Galway.

Constable Whelan, the first casualty of the 1916 rising in Galway.

It is now in the city's museum. The current gravestone was unveiled at the centenary of his birth, and fellow Irish-language poet Máirtín Ó Díreáin gave a speech at its unveiling. The inscription is in the old Gaelic script and may be translated as:

Pádraic Ó Conaire
True Gael and first-rate author

Born 20-2-1882
Died 6-10-1928.

None of the RIC graves in the cemetery have the RIC crest. It was probably not advisable after 1922 when Galway was transformed from a 'shoneen' town to a Republican one. Thirty-four-year-old Constable Patrick Whelan (63409) became the first casualty of the 1916 Rising in Galway when he was shot dead on 26 April. The constabulary had received word that the Volunteers were assembling at Carnmore and went out to confront them. A firefight ensued. Whelan knew many of the Volunteers personally and was ordered to call upon them to surrender. It cost him his life. The RIC retreated and the Volunteers moved towards Oranmore. The inscription on the grave reads: 'Sacred to the memory of Constable Patrick Whelan who died on 26th April 1916 from wounds received while gallantly doing his duty as a member of the Royal Irish Constabulary. Erected by the officers and men of the RIC and many sympathetic friends in the county of Galway WP.'

FORT HILL

Is minic a ligeas béal	The mouth of the grave
na huaighe rud chuig	often allows something to
na truaighde.	go to the mouth of the poor.

SEANFHOCAL/PROVERB

Fort Hill on the shores of Lough Atalia is one the city's oldest graveyards and though still in use, is rarely employed for burials these days. It is a relatively small graveyard, measuring only 2 acres, but thousands are buried here as it used to be the custom in times gone by to put seven or eight bodies in the one plot. It is looked after on a voluntary basis by Tony McDonagh. On the immediate left as you enter the gate is a restored chapel, used once a year for Cemetery Sunday in November. Above the door is a *memento mori* and a Latin inscription which may be translated as follows:

An example of an obelisk at Fort Hill.

This cemetery is dedicated to our Holy Father Augustine
Was opened in the year of our Lord 1500
Enlarged and renovated in the year of our Lord 1852.
Blessed are the dead who died in the Lord.

In 1508, Margaret Athy built a priory dedicated to St Augustine on the hill before the Reformation closed it down and it passed to Galway Corporation. It later became a fortified position from which Red Hugh O'Donnell was repulsed when he tried to sack the city in 1596. The fort was dismantled by the townspeople in 1643 for fear of reprisals its existence might cause and the priory was demolished by Galway Corporation in 1652.

The graveyard wall we see today was built by Robert Hedges Eyre in 1811. The nearby holy well is a remnant of the Augustinians. This private cemetery of Fort Hill dates back to the 1500s but the official burial records of the Augustinian cemetery only go back to the early 1900s. The oldest grave has the following inscription:

> We earnestly beg dear children to say one Ave Maria for the soul of John Bodkin of Anagh, his wife Megg Blake of Ardfry and their prosperity. This is the first tomb made in this abbey in the year 1745.

Fort Hill was the scene of a gruesome mass execution in 1588, when about 300 Spanish sailors, the survivors from the Armada, were beheaded there. After the defeat of the Armada the remnants of the fleet went home by sailing north along the Scottish coastline and down along the Irish coast where they suffered the worst storms in a decade. Their maps of the Irish coastline were inaccurate and about thirty ships were wrecked off the Connacht coast. The *Falco Blanco Mediano* was wrecked off the coast of Clifden and the *Concepión Delcano* ran aground in Mweenish Bay. Survivors from these ships, as well as those who went ashore in Mayo, were brought to Galway where Sir William Fitzwilliam ordered their execution. The Augustinians administered the last rites before they met their grisly end. Some nobles were saved as they could be ransomed. A stone plaque was unveiled to the unfortunate sailors who died here, when La Orden Del Tercio Viejo Del Mar Océano (the Order of the Ocean Sea), the oldest marine corps in the world, founded in 1537, visited the city for the 300th anniversary of the Armada in June 1988.

Spanish plaque to the Armada survivors executed here in 1588.

A plaque with *memento mori* above the chapel at Fort Hill.

Another prominent mass burial was for the victims of the pro-cathedral disaster of 1842 on the corner of Middle Street and Abbeygate Street. Just as the priest was about to celebrate mass, a crack was heard, and the congregation, believing the roof was about to collapse, panicked. Thirty-seven people were killed in the ensuing stampede. Seventeen of the victims were buried on a single day at Fort Hill.

Something I found unusual about Fort Hill was the presence of modern toys on the graves of children who died in the early part of the nineteenth century, such as a gravestone erected by Richard Mortimer in memory of his three children who died in December of 1815. The cemetery contains a First World War grave, that of George Norman from the Claddagh who was an Able Seaman on HMS *Victory*. According to William Henry, author of *Forgotten Heroes*, he died in Kilcock in 1915, after falling from the train whilst returning to his ship from leave in Galway.

RAHOON CEMETERY

Rain on Rahoon falls softly, softly falling,
Where my dark lover lies.
Sad is his voice that calls me, sadly calling,
At grey moonrise.

Love, hear thou
How soft, how sad his voice is ever calling,
Ever unanswered, and the dark rain falling,
Then as now.

Dark too our hearts, O love, shall lie and cold
As his sad heart has lain
Under the moon grey nettles, the black mould
And muttering rain.

'SHE WEEPS OVER RAHOON', JAMES JOYCE

Rahoon Cemetery, also known as Mount St Joseph Cemetery, is located in Westside, to the right before you ascend the hill at Bishop O'Donnell Road. The vandalised ruins of a medieval church surrounded by new houses mark the site of the old Rahoon Graveyard. The old graves themselves, the oldest one dating from 1761, show signs of vandalism. The majority date from the nineteenth century. Few have legible inscriptions.

Not far away is the newer Rahoon Cemetery, which opened in the late nineteenth century. Like the Magdalene Laundry victims, the boys from the Salthill Industrial School, which operated between 1870 and 1995, were only given a headstone in 2013. Before that, their resting place was just an empty patch of ground. Boys were sent there for missing school or if they were unfortunate enough to come from a broken home. The Christian Brothers agreed to manage the school under a committee of laymen and religious staff, and it came under the control of the Department of Education in 1925. According to the Child Abuse Commission's report, the purpose of the school was

A rare Celtic cross in iron.

to take in 'neglected, orphaned, and abandoned Roman Catholic boys, in order to safeguard them from developing criminal tendencies and to prepare them for the world of industry'. Like Letterfrack, it gained a reputation for brutality and child abuse. Indeed, one brother who was removed from Letterfrack due to brutality ended up at the Salthill School, where he continued on where he left off. A comprehensive list of the culprits involved, which makes for disturbing reading, is available for public consumption in the Ryan Report published in 2009. Their mass grave is now marked by a black-marble headstone with gold lettering. Along with their names is the brief inscription, 'Lord have mercy on the souls of the deceased boys of Salthill School'.

In the Griffin family plot, themselves from Rahoon, is the grave of 21-year-old Private Stephen Griffin. He was shot by the Israeli-backed South Lebanon Army in 1980 while serving with the 46th Irish Battalion of UNIFIL. The cemetery also contains a Vietnam War grave, that of Michael Noel Faherty, who was born in Galway on 30 December 1946 and emigrated to America, settling in Marlboro, Massachusetts. He enlisted and fought for his adopted land, and died from a disease he contracted during the war on 5 July 1968. He is also honoured on panel 46 west, line 37 of the Vietnam Veterans Memorial in Washington, DC. For any reader interested in Vietnam War graves I should also mention there is one in Cashel for Marine Peter Nee who was killed in action in Quang Nam on 31 March 1969.

Siobhán MacKenna (1923–86) was born Siobhán Giollamhuire Nic Cionnaith in Belfast into a Catholic nationalist family. She grew up in Galway city, where her father was professor of Mathematics at University College Galway. She was still in her teens when she became a member of an amateur Gaelic theatre group and made her stage debut at Galway's Irish language theatre, the Taibhdhear, before going to the Abbey in 1940. One of her greatest roles was that of Pegeen Mike in *The Playboy of the Western World*. She played the role so well that she overshadowed the main character. She landed an even bigger role in David Lean's blockbuster *Doctor Zhivago* (1965) where she played the role of Anna Gromeko who adopts the main character Yuri Zhivago after the death of his parents. She could have been a bigger star had she moved away from Ireland, but she did not want to

Siobhán MacKenna.

do this. She died of lung cancer in Dublin at the age of 63. The grave is very unassuming. The inscription is in the old Irish script and is shared with that of her mother. Under her name is the single word '*aisteoir*' meaning actress.

Not far away is the grave of Thomas Barnacle, a baker and Nora Barnacle's father, who died in 1921. Aware perhaps of his significance, someone has repainted the inscription in gold to make it stand out. James Joyce, having listened to his muse's tales of her life in Galway, came here to see the graves of her relatives and those close to her. Barnacle had two boyfriends who died within a close time of each other. This inspired Joyce to compose the poem engraved onto the cemetery wall, 'She Weeps over Rahoon', which he wrote in 1913. She had her first boyfriend when she was 13 and 'kept company' with the 16-year-old teacher Michael Feeney, who died of typhoid fever in 1897. In *The Dead*, Greta Conroy hears a song, 'The Lass of Aughrim', which causes her to recall a past love. One of the verses of the song goes as follows:

Oh the rain falls on my heavy locks
And the dew soaks my skin;
My babe lies cold in my arms;
But none will let me in.

When pressed to speak of it, Conroy says: 'He is dead, she said at length. He died when he was only 17. Isn't it terrible thing to die so young as that?'

Michael 'Sonny' Bodkin from Prospect Hill was her next boyfriend and he also died soon after at the age of 20 when he succumbed to TB. The Bodkin tomb, at the top of the hill, is quite large and both Michael and his parents are interred there. A sense of heartbreak from parents who had to bury their son is still felt reading the inscription:

> Erected by Patrick and Winifred Bodkin in loving memory of their dearly beloved son Michael Marin Bodkin who died 11th of February 1900 aged 20 years. Lord Jesus deliver him comfortress of the afflicted and intercede for him. The Lord gave and the Lord hath taken away. Blessed be the name of the Lord.
>
> JOB 1:21.

The tomb of Michael Bodkin.

His mother died in 1915 while his father lived on until 1928. The character of Michael Furey may be a deliberate attempt to fictionalise or a misunderstanding on the part of Joyce. He somehow believed Bodkin was buried in Oughterard and he cycled out there, little realising that he was buried a lot closer to the city. According to *The Dead*, the fictitious Furey was buried in Oughterard where 'his people were from'. Furey died for Conroy. In his play *Exiles* Joyce makes further reference to Bodkin: 'She weeps over Rahoon, over him whom her love has killed, the dark boy whom, as the earth, she embraces in death and disintegration'. *The Dead*, the final story of *Dubliners*, ends with a very beautiful image of Rahoon:

> It [snow] was falling, too, upon every part of the lonely churchyard on the hill where Michael Furey lay buried. It lay thickly drifted on the crooked crosses and headstones, on the spears of the little gate, on the barren thorns. His soul swooned slowly as he heard the snow falling faintly through the universe and faintly falling, like the descent of their last end, upon all the living and the dead.

ST JAMES' CEMETERY

Níl a fhios ag éinne cá bhfuil fód an bháis.	Nobody knows where death will strike.

SEANFHOCAL/PROVERB

Leave the city and follow the old Dublin Road along by Lough Attalia and towards Renmore. A signpost on the left at Mervue will direct

Famine graves.

you from the road. The cemetery is on the right a few yards from the main road. The graveyard was used for burial until the 1950s and fell into disrepair thereafter. It was restored in the 1990s as was the late-medieval church on the site. Is not known for certain where the name comes from, although Galway was a gathering place for pilgrims doing the camino. Another possibility was that James, the patron saint of merchants, was favoured in a city ruled by merchant families. It is a small cemetery and a variety of Galwegians are represented there. The wealthy Wilson Lynch family from Renmore House and the Joyce family of Mervue House have family interred here.

One of the more prominent graves is that of Seán Mulvoy. IRA graves are always prominent in any Irish cemetery. Mulvoy's funeral was said to be one of the largest to take place in St James' Cemetery. He was shot dead on the night of 8 September 1920, while trying to disarm Constable E. Krumm of the Royal Irish Constabulary. Krumm was subsequently shot by IRA man Frank Dowd. After the shooting, the Black and Tans went looking for revenge and took IRA man Seamus Quirke from his lodgings and shot him. Fr Michael Griffin, who himself would soon be dead, administered the last rites. On 10 September 1920, the requiem for both Quirke and Mulvoy was held in the pro-cathedral. Bishop of Galway Dr Thomas O'Dea led 10,000 people and over forty priests in the funeral procession to St James' Cemetery. Seamus Quirke was buried in his native Cork. A new gravestone for Mulvoy was unveiled by Mayor of Galway Michael D. Higgins in 1972.

Buried somewhere in the centre of the graveyard in an unmarked spot is the African-American champion boxer Tom 'The Moor' Molineaux. He died of influenza while visiting Galway on 4 August 1818 and was buried here. He was born in 1784 on a slave plantation in Virginia to a family of fighters. He moved across the Atlantic and arrived in England in 1810, becoming the first black man to fight for the British heavyweight title. He should have won the title but the crowd and umpires were not going to let him and when his opponent Cribb looked defeated, the match was stopped. Officially, this was in response to the accusation that Molineaux had illegally used bullets in his hands to add weight to his punch, but it was obvious that it was really to give his opponent a chance to recover, and Cribb managed to win. Around

The grave of Seán Mulvoy.

1816, Molineaux arrived in Dublin, by which time his career was in decline and he had descended into alcoholism. He toured the country demonstrating his skills and died aged 34 of liver failure in a room occupied by the band of the 77th Regiment. He died forgotten and alone, far from home. There is no plaque to him.

Not far from the cemetery, on the shores of Lough Atalia, just beside the railway bridge on the Renmore side, is a plain wooden cross. It marks the spot where a 17-year-old Swiss student, Manuela Riedo, was murdered on her third day in Galway in 2007. The murder shocked the nation. Indeed, had the judiciary system not been so lenient, the murder could have been avoided. The killer, local man Gerald Barry, was 'known to the Gardaí'. Although he had a very violent criminal record he was continually given another chance. At 17, he was involved in the fatal assault of 26-year-old Colm Phelan from Tipperary, who was in Galway on a stag when he was attacked by Barry and his friends. Barry pleaded guilty to manslaughter and was sentenced to five years, of which he only served two, which left him free to offend again. He was the main suspect in the rape of a French girl and was on bail for assaulting his partner when he murdered Manuela Riedo. The simple cross just says 'Manuela'.

A memorial cross erected to murdered Swiss student, Manuela Riedo.

ROSCAM

Roscam is on the Galway to Oranmore coast road, on the right-hand side as you pass over the railway line. There is very little to see here unless you know exactly what you are looking for. The site has bullaun stones, depressions in rocks that were known for their curative properties. Local lore has it that St Patrick used them for absolutions. The monastic settlement there is believed to have been set up by St Odran, a brother of St Ciarán, in the sixth century, and destroyed by Viking raiders in 807. The graveyard, sometimes known as The Moor (from the Irish '*muir*' meaning sea) is on private farmland and is the oldest Christian burial ground within the city limits. Many of the graves have no decipherable inscription anymore. An ancient church and the remains of a round tower, built between 900 and 1200, are still visible. It contains a recumbent, or horizontal, grave slab adorned with a cross that can be dated to around the fifteenth century. Another example of a recumbent grave slab in the city is the 'Crusader's' grave in the church of St Nicholas. The graveyard was used extensively in the famine period. It has several low, uncut stones, typical of the peasantry until the late nineteenth century.

THE ABBEY

'Our dead are never dead to us, until we have forgotten them.'

GEORGE ELIOT

The Franciscans have been in the city for around 700 years and their monks are a familiar presence, easily recognisable by their brown habit. To the rear of the early nineteenth-century church on Francis Street is the remains of a graveyard, the final resting place of many of Galway's ruling merchant families. When the parliamentarian soldiers ransacked the city in 1652, they opened the graves hoping to find treasures. The corpses were thrown around and left to the dogs. Around 1655, the same time the

Tribes of Galway were ordered out of the city, the graveyard was cleared away by Mathew Quin. The abbey was demolished and the gravestones removed. Despite this, fragments of some of the graves remain and the opulence of Galway's past shines through. A fragment of the tomb of Sir Peter Ffrench and his wife Maria can be dated to the late sixteenth century. Local lore claims that Colonel Stubbers made chimney pieces from part of the tomb. Also imbedded in the modern concrete wall, adorned with a sword motif, is the De Burgo memorial with a sword erected by Father Valentine Blake in 1645.

One of the more famous burials there was that of James Hardiman (1782–1855), librarian at Queen's College, Galway and after whom the current university library has been named. He was a noted historian and wrote *A History of the Town and County of Galway* in 1820. Not even such a distinguished scholar as he could get in the way of progress, however, and the modern building to the rear of the abbey was probably built on his grave. A blue plaque at the rear entrance reminds the visitor that he was interred there.

The remnant of an old tomb at the rear of the abbey on Francis Street.

THE CLADDAGH GRAVEYARD

Good friend, for Jesus' sake forbear,
To dig the dust enclosed here.
Blest be the man that spares these stones,
And cursed be he that moves my bones.

WILLIAM SHAKESPEARE

A *memento mori*, dating from 1488 at the entrance to Claddagh graveyard.

A *memento mori* dating from 1488 with the quote from the Book of Job 'I know that I will arise and see my God' imbedded on the graveyard wall greets the visitor. Another interesting feature was a tree growing from a grave. Where there is death, there is life. Although hundreds of famine victims were buried here, there is no monument to them. Were it not for the Claddagh Church Cemetery Book, which in neat handwriting recorded those buried there during this turbulent period in the city's history, their burial would have been extinguished from memory.

The earliest headstone is believed to date back to the sixteenth century. Also here is the tomb of Bishop O'Donnell, the second Bishop of Galway, who died in June of 1855 after ten years in office. A road in Rahoon is named after him. Much of the old cemetery was removed when the fire station was built in 1957. According to local lore, there was considerable poltergeist activity when the dead were disturbed.

The tomb of Bishop O'Donnell.

ST NICHOLAS' COLLEGIATE CHURCH

> They shall grow not old, as we that are left grow old:
> Age shall not weary them, nor the years condemn.
> At the going down of the sun and in the morning,
> We will remember them.
>
> LAURENCE BINYON, 'ODE TO THE FALLEN'

The church of St Nicholas in the heart of Galway is the oldest church in the city, dating mostly from 1320. Unfortunately, we know very little about the early history of the church and surrounding graveyard. In his history of the church from 1912, Revd Fleetwood Berry summed up its turbulent past by stating the following:

> If the old stones of St Nicholas' Collegiate Church could speak, what strange tales they would tell of war and peace, of prosperity and adversity, of civil and religious strife, of self-denying devotion to the service of God, and rash sacrilegious spoliation.

When the church was built, Galway was a tiny, very new town, an English colonial outpost surrounded by the Gaelic Irish, a sort of frontier settlement in the Wild West. The merchants thought highly of themselves and Dominick Lynch, Mayor of Galway in 1486, spent a great deal of money enlarging the church to display their wealth and power. By the standards of the time it was almost as big as a cathedral. A system of churchwardens was created in 1484. They were drawn from one of the ruling merchant families, with Stephen Lynch becoming the first one, having been appointed by Pope Innocent VIII. Among Catholics, this system lasted until 1832.

The Lynch window marks the spot where James Lynch Fitz-Stephen, who died in 1519, is supposed to be buried. He became infamous for hanging his own son in the late fifteenth century, an event that may or may not have actually happened. The faces of the angels have been vandalised. This is believed to have happened when Cromwellian troops used the church as a stable in 1652 and they

had little regard for either the Catholic or Anglican Church. Across from the Lynch window is the eagle representing the Browne family. These coats of arms can be seen all over the medieval city. The oldest gravestone is a recumbent grave slab, dating from around 1280, which predates the church. Decorated with a cross, it is the only gravestone of its kind west of the Shannon, with a Norman French inscription

Above: The Lynch window.
Left: The 'Crusader's' grave.

on the edge that can be translated as 'Here lies Adam (or Alfin?) Bure. May God have mercy on his soul. Whoever will pray for his soul will have twenty days' indulgence'. Though it is labelled the 'Crusader's' grave, it may not have any links to the crusaders at all. It has been suggested that a Templar church once stood on the site until it was demolished in 1324. A tombstone lying on the floor of the south aisle has three Maltese crosses in the centre and as well as an anchor. James Berry Wood, writing in 1912 could make out the following inscription: 'Here lieth the body of … Fizttheig and Elyn Linch his wife … 1566.'

The bubonic plague is known to have struck Galway in 1629, but there is no memorial to those who died during this time. One of the most famous wardens was John Bodkin, who in 1691 was forced to hand over the church. As he did so he proclaimed that his hand would not decompose while the church was in Anglican hands. He died in 1710 and even though the church was no longer Catholic, the wardens continued to be buried there, and though his coffin rotted, his body remained undecomposed and was still in this state in 1838, which caused much commotion. For fear of the prophecy, the body was vandalised and the hand chopped off and stolen. The theft was denounced in the *Galway Weekly Advertiser* of 1838 and the hand was eventually returned. The tomb, located near the altar, was sealed, and nothing more was heard of it. I wrote about this unusual occurrence in my book *Fadó Fadó More Tales of Lesser Known Irish History* and I note many guidebooks neglect to mention it, leaving some to wonder whether it ever happened at all.

The Eyre family, after whom Eyre Square is named, is well commemorated in the church. John Eyre from Wiltshire came to Galway with the Cromwellian conquest and smashed the power of the tribes of Galway, ensuring Protestant dominance of the city for the next 200 years. Edward Eyre, Mayor of Galway, is buried here, and his plaque reads as follows:

> Here lyeth interred the body of Edward Eyre Esq., son of Giles Eyre Esq., of Brickworth in Wiltshire near Salisbury with five of his children 3 sons and 5 daughters. He deceased the 14th April 1683.

Also commemorated is Jane Eyre, a 'virtuous and pious parishioner', who in 1760 bequeathed £300 to the corporation to give bread to thirty-six 'poor objects' forever.

The wall plaques give the visitor an insight into how the people died. One tells of how a 22-year-old ensign, George Frederick de Carteret, died by drowning after falling into the poorly lit docks in 1843, while another tells of how 11-year-old James Kearney was playing with his spinning top in the street when he was run over by a horse and cart. The gravestone of Elizabeth Kingcorne, who died in 1684, bears the following epitaph, 'the shortest life, the longest rest, God takes them sovnest whom he loveth best.'

The church has numerous brass plaques to officers who died in India. In the British Army of the nineteenth century, an officer made a career by buying his way up the ladder or serving time in places such as India. The 88th Regiment of Foot (Connaught Rangers) or The Devil's Own was raised in 1793 as the threat of a French invasion loomed. They were recruited mostly from the west and were stationed

Church of Ireland churches have memorial plaques which inform about the circumstances under which the deceased passed away, in this case a young boy.

at what is now Renmore Barracks. They fought against Napoleon in Spain and against the Russians in the Crimea. On 28 June 1920 some of its members started a mutiny in the Punjab which led to the execution of Private James Daly. Some accounts suggest Daly may have been a Galwegian but he himself claimed allegiance to Tyrellspass. The graves of the Connaught Rangers are widespread. About 2,500 of them fell in the First World War, and while a few of their graves are in the county, such as at New Cemetery, Creagh Cemetery and Kilmacduagh, most are buried at Grangegorman Military Cemetery, Dublin, France, Belgium, Germany, Greece, Turkey, Bulgaria, Egypt, Palestine, India, Iran, Iraq, Israel, and England. In 1966, a stained-glass memorial window to the Connaught Rangers was included in the new Galway Cathedral.

A Celtic cross in the corner is the sole sign of recognition in the city to the fallen of the First World War. Approximately 683 Galwegians fell in the conflict. The names inscribed are in memory of some of those who are buried where they fell. At the bottom is the inscription: 'Pass not this shrine in sorrow but in pride and may you live as nobly as they died'.

A Freemason grave.

A *memento mori* beneath the window where Mayor Lynch is reputed to have hanged his own son.

While monuments to the fallen are possible in other parts of the country such as Wexford, Dublin and Cahir, it is seemingly still not possible to do this in Galway and any such monument will remain hidden away for the foreseeable future.

There are quite a few interesting graves outside. There is, for example, one with Freemason symbols. The first of the three symbols is the universal Freemason symbol of the compass and the square with a G, symbolising God and geometry in the centre. The other two mystified me so I contacted the Freemasons, and archivist Rebecca Hayes told me that the Star of David is referred to as the Seal of Solomon and is considered the most important symbol of Royal Arch masonry, while the arch symbolises the arch of heaven, again associated with Royal Arch masonry which promotes the Freemason to four degrees. The graveyard also contains the grave of a Poor Law inspector, Major Patrick McKie, who died of the fever during the Great Famine in 1849. Reference on the gravestone is made to 'The Buffs', which was the nickname for the East Kent Regiment, in which he served. The gravestones hint at where business was booming in the eighteenth century and a gravestone makes reference to Jamaica, a place which made a fortune for many of the merchant families.

Granite cenotaph to a tragedy on the Corrib.

A large granite obelisk in memory of a boating tragedy on the Corrib in 1887 was erected to the right of the side door with the Claddagh ring and a *memento mori* as symbols. The following is engraved:

> To the memory of John Skelton Thomson, Francis John Kinkead and Thomas Leopold Roberts who all perished in Lough Corrib, 17th August 1887. Moved with pity for so sad a catastrophe the Citizens of Galway had this Monument erected. They were lovely and pleasant in their lives and in death they were not divided.

Just outside the church railings is the famous Lynch memorial window, allegedly where Mayor Lynch hanged his own son, in reality a nineteenth-century mélange of medieval Galway artefacts. It does, however, have an interesting *memento mori*, dating from 1524 with the inscription, now hardly legible: 'Remember Deathe Vaniti of Vaniti and all is but Vaniti'.

CLAREGALWAY

God's finger touched him and he slept.

LORD ALFRED TENNYSON

The Francisan friary was built by John de Cogan around 1252. It contains a nice example of a canopy tomb, the resting place of a Burke (also known as De Burgo or in Irish De Búrca). Their coat of arms, with the date 1648, is clearly seen over the tomb. After the Suppression the friary was granted to Richard de Burgo in 1570. The friars were allowed to remain in or near the buildings but were driven out in 1589 by Sir Richard Bingham who then converted the buildings into barracks. The tomb of Martin D'Arcy and family dating from 1780 is also visible, tucked away into a niche. A white-marble plaque within the ruins requests the visitor to say 'a pater or ave for a poor soul suffering in purgatory'.

Canopy tomb showing the Burke coat of arms at Claregalway friary.

Just inside the entrance, inscribed in the old Irish script, is a Celtic cross marking the grave of Tom Ruane, captain of the Second Western Division IRA from 1916 to 1920. He fought in 1916 and was imprisoned in Frongoch. He later fought with the anti-Treaty IRA and died in 1937.

THE PRISON CROSS

The Law must take its course.

RESPONSE OF THE LORD LIEUTENANT TO AN APPEAL FOR CLEMENCY FOR MYLES JOYCE

It is an unassuming cross in the cathedral's car park and it's easy to miss, yet it forms the last resting place of those who were executed or died in the old Galway Gaol (1818–1940), which occupied the space where the cathedral and car park now stand. No names are inscribed on the cross, and while most of the convicts were doubtlessly guilty of murder, some were also innocent. The inscription, in both Irish and English, reads as follows: 'This marks the burial place of all those who died or were executed in Old Gaol of Galway (1810–1939) on which the cathedral now stands. Eternal rest grant unto them o Lord.'

As Ireland had no hangman of its own, many famous English hangmen such as William Marwood plied their trade in Galway. William Calcraft preceded Marwood and served between 1829 and 1874, but it is not known if he operated in Galway. Prior to the construction of Galway Gaol, executions were held at Gallows Green, close to where the Liam Mellows monument now stands. There were still public executions until 1868. In his death sentence speech, the judge often solemnly declared that the prisoner would be taken to a place of execution where they would be hanged 'until they were dead'. A quick death was not deemed relevant or humane and many hangings were slow and agonising. The condemned man often tipped the hangman so he would speed the process. Marwood became hangman in 1872 and changed this. He was passionate about his job and once remarked, 'I have studied my profession so that a man dies at my hands with as little pain as I give myself by touching the back of my hand with my finger'. He was also the first British executioner to conduct his hangings behind prison walls. He perfected the 'long drop' method, which took the prisoner's weight, height and physical stature into consideration and introduced the free-running noose instead of the crude hangman's knot. It was certainly an improvement on the 'short drop' which often led to slow strangulation. The execution chamber at Galway Gaol was above the main doorway, roughly where the entrance to the cathedral's car park is. The following are the details of some of those buried under the prison cross.

On 3 April 1835 Richard Halloran was hanged for the murder of Richard Burke. In August Patrick Meany and John McDermott were hanged for the murder of David Ormsby, and later that month Michael Ryan was executed for the murder of his wife Honor. On 3 May 1839 John Manion was hanged for the murder of Thomas Mulkere. Unfortunately, little seems to be known about the circumstances of these executions. On 14 April 1841 Patrick McHugh was executed for the murder of David Fenrick. On 3 September 1849, Patrick Cormick was hanged for the murder of Miss Prendergast at Portumna.

John Hurley was hanged for the murder of 16-year-old Catherine Kendrigan on 27 August 1853. Kendrigan from Kilyullagh was a servant in William Connors' shebeen. He sent her shopping for food in Loughrea. As she reached the bridge at Toolooubaune, she met Hurley of Bookeen. Twenty-four-year-old Hurley had been in Connors' employment but had been dismissed due to dishonesty. Screams were heard from the bridge and Kendrigan's body was later discovered by Constable George Humphries covered with hay on the edge of Dunsandle Wood. Suspicion immediately fell on Hurley who had suddenly come into wealth and was arrested but managed to escape. Hurley spent several weeks on the run before he was eventually caught sleeping in a field. When the death sentence was read out

The Prison Cross. The final resting place for those who died or were put to death in Galway Gaol.

after a six-hour trial, he declared his innocence, and cried for vengeance upon both judge and jury, either in this world, or in that to come. The execution was delayed until 6 p.m., lest a reprieve be granted and delivered by train, but none came. He eventually acknowledged his guilt as he stood on the trapdoor. As executions were still public at the time, his was witnessed by several people, including women and children, who regarded it as a 'serious amusement'. He was given a drop of 7½ feet, but it failed to kill him and he strangled to death at the end of the rope, shaken by convulsions. One of the witnesses was a professor of anatomy at Queen's College, Galway – Charles Croker King. He subsequently wrote a detailed account of the execution for the 1854 *Dublin Quarterly Journal of Medical Science*.

On 16 January 1880 Martin M'Hugo was executed for the murder of Michael Breheny. The victim's body was found battered with a stone in a laneway at Woodford. Hugo was immediately suspected as it was known that he had been involved in a dispute with the deceased only a month previously. Breheny could only use his left arm and was ill-matched, though he managed to rip off a piece of his attacker's coat, which matched a hole in M'Hugo's. Nevertheless it took three trials before his guilt could be established and he was hanged by Marwood.

The Land War was particularly vicious in the Galway area, where bitter fighting over land ownership too place. Patrick Walsh was hanged on 22 September 1882 for murdering Martin Lydon at Bannogaes, Letterfrack on the night of 24 April 1881 when, with eight men, he stormed his cottage. Lydon died immediately but his son lived long enough to identify his assailants. The killings did not stop there. A leading witness for the prosecution of the murders was Constable Kavanagh. He was shot dead outside Letterfrack Barracks on 15 February 1882. Walsh's brother, Michael, was tried, found guilty and sentenced to death, but had it commuted to penal servitude. On 15 January 1883, Patrick Higgins and Michael Flynn were executed for the murder of Joseph and John Huddy.

There were bound to be miscarriages of justice and the most notable one was the case of Myles Joyce, perhaps the greatest injustice in Irish legal history. In the village of Maamtrasna, close to the Mayo border, an entire family was murdered in 1882. This shocked the nation and justice was demanded. The trial was held at Greenstreet Court in Dublin and left a lot to be desired. While some of the defendants could understand English, the Dublin accent and the legalese in which the trial was conducted baffled them. Myles Joyce spoke no English and was defended by an English-speaking solicitor. Even though part of the proceedings were translated for him by an RIC man, this was done in Donegal Irish, which he would not have completely understood. Patrick Joyce and Pat Casey admitted their guilt but swore that Myles Joyce was innocent. In all, eight people were convicted for the murders and three sentenced to hang. Of those who served the twenty years' penal servitude it is believed some were also innocent. Some of the accused only pleaded guilty under pressure from their local priest, Father Michael McHugh. Appeals for clemency were made to Earl Spencer, the lord lieutenant of Ireland. His curt response became infamous – 'the Law must take its course'. According to Jarlath Waldron, who wrote a book about the murders in 1992, the scaffolding on which the three condemned men were hanged was on the very spot where the prison cross now lies. On the day of the execution, Joyce addressed the assembled journalists, some of whom understood Irish and translated his words as follows:

> I am going. Why should I die? I am not guilty. I had neither hand nor foot in the murder. I know nothing about it; but God forgive them that swore my life away. It is a poor thing to die on a stage for what I never did. God help my wife and her five orphans. I had no hand, act nor part in it; but I have my priest with me. I am as innocent as the child in the cradle.

He was still talking and moving his head when Marwood fixed the noose and pulled the lever. The three bodies fell. Two of the ropes were still but Joyce still moved. The execution had been botched and it was several minutes before he died. The bodies were thrown into a quicklime grave. Marwood later lied to journalists when he said the execution had gone well, and remarked about Joyce: 'He was a wild bad-looking fellow and kept jabbering and talking. I couldn't understand a word of his "lingo"'.

The black flag was raised over the prison to announce to the assembled mourners outside that the grisly deed had been performed. The controversy continued and soldiers on duty at Galway Gaol claimed to have seen the ghost of Myles Joyce a few nights later, which further fuelled the notion of injustice. Two years later, in August 1884, Dr John Mac Evilly, the Archbishop of Tuam, came to Tourmakeady to hold a Confirmation ceremony. As he did so, Tom Casey, who had given evidence against Joyce, came into the church, walked up to the altar and declared he was to blame for the men being hanged and that the evidence he had given was false. He might have done this out of guilt or because he had had an argument with the Crown over payment. Myles Joyce is still, to this day, listed as a murderer.

Another hangman who provided his services to Galway Gaol was James Berry (1852–1913) who operated between 1884 and 1891. He hanged Michael Downey on 16 January 1885. Downey had murdered a farmer, John Moylan of Clonboo. Moylan was out walking with his wife when he was approached by four men who shot him dead for no apparent reason. The RIC thought Downey was having an affair with Moylan's wife. Though the RIC believed he had fired the fatal shot, Downey denied doing so and was tried three times before being found guilty. On the eve of his execution he admitted to the murder. Four days later Berry hanged Thomas Parry for the murder of Alice Burns. Parry had shot her after she broke up with him. He was a tortured soul and before his execution he handed the prison governor a note, which went:

> I wish to assure the public and family and friends that I was of unsound mind for a week previous to the murder and for some time afterwards. I am happy to suffer for the crime which I committed and confident that I shall enter upon an eternity of bliss. I die at peace with all men and hope that anyone I have ever injured will forgive me.

With the exception of Thomas Keeley, there were no hangings in Galway Gaol in the twentieth century. Keeley was hanged for the murder of his landlady, Mary Clasby, on 23 April 1902. Keeley, a painter, shared a house with Clasby in North Gate Street, Athenry. While drinking one night, they quarrelled and he hit her on the head with his painter's hammer and killed her. Keeley was hanged by William Billington. Hangings thereafter seem to have only been performed at Mountjoy. The more infamous hangman, Pierrepoint, who plied his trade from the 1920s onwards, did not execute anyone here, and by the time he arrived the gaol was closing down.

THE CATHEDRAL CRYPT

De mortuis	Of the dead say
nil nisi bonum.	nothing but good.

HORACE

Underneath Galway Cathedral is a crypt containing the mortal remains of four of the bishops of Galway starting in 1888, which pre-dated the cathedral by several decades. Not all the bishops of Galway are buried here, and Bishop O'Donnell, for example, who reigned between 1844 and his death in 1855, is buried in the Claddagh Graveyard.

Few bishops attracted as much attention as Bishop Michael Browne (1895–1980) and any Galwegian who lived during his reign will have their own story to tell about him. He was born in Westport and became Bishop of Galway in 1937, which made him the most powerful man in the city. He was instrumental in helping the survivors of the *Athenia* who came to Galway in 1939, having been torpedoed by the Germans. Together with Bishop McQuaid of Dublin he helped defeat the Family Planning Bill, which saw the demise of Noel Browne and supported the infamous boycott of Protestants in the Wexford village of Fethard-on-Sea. His crowning achievement was the cathedral built on the site of the old gaol. Its architecture is unusual; an underestimated gem, and it was referred to by Galwegians as Taj Micheáil. Bishop Michael Browne features in Brendan Ó hEithir's best-selling novel *Lig Sinn i gCathú* (Deliver

Memorial window for the Connaught Rangers at the cathedral, the only memorial in the whole county in a Catholic place of worship to those who fought in the British Army.

Plaque to Bishop Browne, the man behind Galway's cathedral.

us into Temptation), which deals with Galway of the late 1940s in the guise of the fictitious Ballycastle.

CASTLELAWN CEMETERY

Directions: Travel along the Dyke Road and take the first right after the hill. Then as you move downhill along Coolough Road take the second right, which brings you into Castlelawn Heights Estate. Proceed up the hill until you come to a green with the lisheen on your right.

The cemetery has different names. I grew up referring to it simply as 'the cemetery'. Older residents, however, called it 'the lisheen'. There is another cemetery called lisheen at Ballybrit and Castlegar. A lisheen was a sacred place where it was usual to bury unbaptised children. The place was not to be tampered with, and often believed to be protected by otherworldly powers such as the *sí* or the faerie. It was considered unlucky to build too close to a lisheen, and maybe for this reason that most of the houses are built at least 100 yards from it. The landscape there has changed dramatically as the urban sprawl enveloped farmland. It is marked on Ordnance Survey maps from the nineteenth century. It is believed that there was poltergeist activity in a house close to it. A similar case of poltergeist activity occurred in Rahoon when new houses were built over a baby's grave.

The oldest marked graves do not seem to predate 1900 but there are many more people interred here than it would seem. Uninscribed and uncarved stones were used as grave markers up until the twentieth century, probably for reasons of poverty as few could afford a decent headstone with a nice inscription for their loved one.

MENLO

Life levels all men. Death reveals the eminent.

GEORGE BERNARD SHAW

Menlo is a quiet village, only 2 miles from the city centre, on the banks of the Corrib, and has been settled since the earliest times as the collapsed-portal Dolmen, the only one within the city limits, shows. For centuries the Blakes, one of the tribes of Galway, ruled here, and their ancestors lie in the small, peaceful graveyard behind the pier. The Blakes have long associations with the city dating as far back as 1303, when Richard Blake was made sheriff of Connacht. Their original castle was at the foot of Quay Street. In addition to Menlo, the Blakes has estates at Ardfry, Ballyglunin, Furbo and Anbally. The graveyard is marked on the Ordnance Survey map of 1840 as a lisheen, a sacred place. Menlo Castle, where the Blakes resided, was built by Sir Valentine Blake (1560–1635) in 1622, when he was raised to the peerage of baronet. The oldest grave in the cemetery is that of Elizabeth Donelan of Spiddal, who had married into the Blake family, and dates from 1822. The inscription reads:

> Here rests the body of Mrs Ellis Donelan relecit of J Donelan Esquire. She died August 20th 1822 aged 66. Sincereley & deservedly regretted by her family and friends may she rest in peace amen.

Sir Valentine Blake MP, also known as 'Sunday Boy', died in 1847, aged 66. He had received the moniker on account of being confined to his castle, where a summons could not be served, to avoid creditors. Nor indeed could it be served on a Sunday, the day he ventured out of the castle to socialise, making sure he was back before midnight, sometimes with creditors in pursuit. When he ran for re-election he campaigned from a boat in Woodquay, as apparently a summons could not be served on water either. He was elected to parliament in 1812 and took part in the struggle for Catholic Emancipation. According to local newspaper reports of the time, his remains were deposited in the family vault at Menlo, but this does not appear to be marked in the graveyard. It seems odd that a family as powerful as the Blakes did not have their own mausoleum. I came across a long-forgotten and neglected man-made structure in the woods, to the right of the main driveway, on a small hill overlooking the Corrib, about 200 yards away from the castle. This is where, I believe, the family vault was. In shape, it certainly bore a strong resemblance to many burial vaults I had seen in the county, and having been dug into the hill it is probably much bigger than it looks. It has no inscription, but this is not unusual. Another possibility is that it is one of the square plots surrounded by kerbstone, but nothing else. There is a similar-size plot in Clonbern to the Browne family, but the Browne plot has cast-iron railings and this plot is devoid of any ornamentation. As such, the Blakes of the nineteenth century are among the very few landlords in the county without a splendid monument marking their final resting place.

Sir Thomas Blake succeeded his father in 1847. His funeral in January of 1875, when he was waked for four days and four nights, proved controversial. Sir Thomas was Catholic and a regular mass goer, but his son, Sir Valentine, refused to acknowledge this and had him buried as a Protestant. The tenants also believed Sir Thomas to be Catholic, and when they saw the Protestant minister at the graveside a riot broke out. It was somewhat similar to when a Burke of Glinsk, related to Thomas Henry Burke, was being buried in Tuam in 1838: a riot broke out as the mourners believed he was a Catholic and took umbrage at the sight of the Protestant clergyman at the graveside. In the ensuing melee, his father, Major William Burke, was pushed into his son's grave. Again, this grave is not marked.

Sir Valentine was not popular, and 'Blake style of living' became a byword in the county for those who aped the English and lived irresponsible, extravagant lives. When he died, his estate amounted to less than £3,000, a meagre sum for a man of his position. His second daughter, Florence Anne (1866–1899) was married in 1896 to Captain Norton, Clowes Castle (died 1930) of the Royal Irish Regiment, eldest son of Charles Castle of Hawford, Worcester, but died just three years later and was buried at Menlo.

The castle was accidentally destroyed by fire on the night of 26 July 1910. Sir Valentine and his wife were in Dublin at the time of the fire but their daughter Eleanor, born in 1865 and an invalid, confined to her bed by rheumatism, was at home, and it was in her room that the fire started. Also in the house were two maids, Anne Browne and Delia Early and the groom, James Kirwan. By the time the maids noticed the fire, it had engulfed the stairs, and they

The grave of Sir Valentine Blake.

An cenotaph commemorating the fire of 1910 with the ruins of Menlo Castle in the background.

climbed onto the roof. Kirwan climbed down the ivy. Early jumped from the roof and was killed in the fall when she landed on her head. Browne followed her, and though badly injured in the fall, she survived and later emigrated to America. No trace of Eleanor Blake was ever found. A polished granite obelisk was erected on the edge of the woods to her memory. The inscription reads:

> To the memory of Eleanor Camilla Eliza Blake who perished in the disastrous fire at Menlo Castle July 26th 1910 aged 48 Years. This memorial is affectionately dedicated by her loving brother T Blake. Thy will be done.

T. Blake refers to Lieutenant Thomas Patrick Ulick John Harvey Blake (1870–1925). Though it was announced later that year that the castle was to be rebuilt, this never happened and it remains a picturesque, crumbling ruin.

There was a considerable RIC presence at the funeral of Sir Valentine in 1912. The locals had not forgotten his father's funeral and local *seanchaí*, or storyteller, Tomás Ó Laighleis said that his gravestone was erected over his feet as an insult. He was succeeded by his eldest son, Thomas. His widow, Dame Camilla, survived him until 4 March 1929. One of the last prominent Blakes was Henry St John Blake (1891–1957) who is also buried here.

There are a great deal more people buried at Menlo than it would appear. In times gone by, farmers would commemorate their dead with a simple unmarked stone. One of the many unmarked graves is that of James Ward, the gatekeeper, pictured in Maurice Semple's *Reflections on the Corrib* (1974). Although there is a Ward plot and one of the family members, Michael Ward, died in 1925, there is no mention of James Ward on the gravestone. Ward was shot dead at the gate lodge on 7 February 1925. He left behind two children and his widow believed he was murdered over a land-related issue. Although five farmers' sons from Menlo village were arrested – John Moloney, Patrick Moloney, Luke Fahy, James Fahy and Denis Duggan – a jury decreed that Ward had been 'wilfully murdered by some person or persons unknown'.

MERLIN PARK WOODS

Directions: Travelling along the Dublin Road out of the city, Merlin Park Hospital is on the left. The graves are located in a hollow behind the Imaging building.

The ancient Merlin Park Woods, which diminished greatly in size during the Celtic Tiger years to make way for property, have an interesting pair of graves side by side. In the seventeenth century, there was

Graves in Merlin Park Woods.

an inn and thoroughfare there. According to local folklore, an elderly Irish-speaking couple lived there. A Cromwellian soldier came by and asked for a cup of water. It is possible that the current name of the area, Dougiska, comes from the Irish *deoch uisce*, a drink of water, though it could also be *dubh uisce*, meaning 'black water'. The couple did not understand English and the soldier thought they were refusing him and murdered them both. The inscription 'Conor O'Reillie 1650' was at one stage legible. The larger stone is inscribed with a cross and carvings such as blacksmith's tools, suggestive perhaps of the deceased's occupation. The smaller grave slab just has a cross.

BUSHYPARK

Directions: Bushypark Church is about 4 kilometres from the city on the left as you head out along the N59 towards Clifden. It is worth a visit for its famine graves, low, uncut fieldstones to the rear of the church, and also for the tomb of Revd John Roche, who died in the famine in 1847.

Famine graves at Bushypark. Simple uncarved stones marked the final resting places of many poor farmers until the twentieth century.

At the gable end of the church are steps leading down into the sealed crypt of the Blake-Forsters. Their family history is carved on huge stone slabs that display their family crest and have not eroded with the passing of time. The highly legible inscription of the stone plaques reveals the origin of the family name. The Forsters were decedents of Baldwin I of Flanders who died in Arras in 877. They came to England after the Battle of Hastings and Galway in the seventeenth century when a Captain Francis Forster married Mary, daughter of Sir James O'Donnellan, son of the last chief of Clanbrasal. Within the crypt are the remains of Francis Blake-Forster and his son Charles. Captain Francis Blake-Forster served with the Connaught Rangers. He was arrested in 1854 for planning a duel

Revd John Roche, one of many priests who died during the famine.

with John Stratford Kirwan of Moyne. Though duels were always illegal, the law was rarely enforced. By the mid-nineteenth century, however, the RIC were cracking down on the practice. The captain's son, Charles, (1851–1874) was born on the site of what is now the Forster Court Hotel on Forster Street. He was equally passionate about duelling, believing it to be part of a young gentleman's upbringing. After being educated in England he returned to Galway and became a town councillor and eventually, in 1874, high sheriff. He also had a passion for writing and composed a number of pieces on the history of Galway for the *Galway Vindicator* and the *Galway Express* between 1869 and 1871. In 1872, he wrote his *magnum opus*, *The Irish Chieftains, or, a struggle for the Crown*, an account of the Williamite War from the Galway perspective. Its publication caused a stir as the cover controversially contained an image of the harp without the crown. He was expelled from all the county clubs as a result. It is believed that he wrote much more, but his writings disappeared after his early death, caused by a brain haemorrhage brought on by overwork when he was just 23.

6

WEST GALWAY

Muintir an Iarthar,	The people of the west are
's iad cairde mo chroí	the friends of my heart
Fáilte is féile a bheidh romham	I will be welcomed and
ar ghach taobh	entertained from all sides
Ar fhágáil an tsaoil seo,	On leaving this life,
's é ghuím ar an Rí	I pray to the lord
Gur leo sinn a	That I may be interred
shínfear i gcill mé.	with them.
Trasna na Tonnta	Trasna na Tonnta

'ACROSS THE WAVES', A TRADITIONAL FOLK SONG

GALWAY BAY

Oh, wild and cold the cruel sea,
That keeps my love so long from me!
Alone I stand upon the shore,
And hear no voice but the ocean's roar.
My eyes are dim and my heart is sore,
Watching and waiting for you ashore.

A CLEGGAN WOMAN'S LAMENT, AGNES LYNAM, 1927

Galway Bay was for those living on the coast what the field was to the farmer and it sometimes took their lives.

The majestic Galway Bay is itself a massive graveyard and its waters, used largely today for recreational activities, have a darker, more cruel side. In times gone by, the bay was to the men of the Claddagh and other coastal villages the equivalent of what a field was to a farmer. The sea sometimes took their lives and the bodies of drowned

Monument to the fishing men of the Claddagh who died tragically in 1902.

fishermen could at times be identified by the pattern on their Aran pullovers. The Claddagh, from the Irish *cladach*, meaning rocky seashore, was the closest fishing village to Galway city. A monument on the quay recalls a disaster that took the lives of eight Claddagh fishermen on 4 May 1902. They set out for Kilcolgan Point, and half a mile from Tawin their boat capsized, more than likely while they were lashing the sail to the mast. The villagers of Tawin had no boats available and looked on in helpless horror. The following men drowned: Patrick Folan, Patrick Burns, Patrick Walsh, Patrick McDonagh, John Barrett, Michael Burke, Michael Dwyer and Stephen Hynes. A ninth man, Patrick Walsh, swam ashore at Kilcolgan, but died of exhaustion on the beach. I could not find their graves and it is possible that they were removed when Galway Fire Station was built on part of the graveyard in 1956.

As the Battle for the Atlantic raged not far from the Irish coast, it was inevitable that Galway would experience something of the Second World War and a number of planes, both Allied and Axis, crashed into the bay. On 22 October 1940, a Focke-Wulf FW 200 from Kampfgeschwader (squadron) number 40 crashed into the Atlantic near Clifden. Two bodies were washed ashore at Letermara. The men were identified as 27-year-old Oberleutnant Theophil Schuldt from Eisenach and Dr Johannes Sturm from Haag. Both were buried at Glencree War Cemetery in Wicklow in plots 51 and 50 respectively. The bodies of the rest of the crew were never recovered. Their names were:

Feldwebel (Sergeant) Walter Berghaus
Feldwebel Friedrich Gruber
Feldwebel Friedrich Ploeger
Gefreiter (Private) Walter Grassel

On 12 March 1941 an Armstrong Whitworth AW38 Whitley from RAF 502 Squadron based in Aldergrove, County Antrim crashed into the bay while returning from a convoy night-escort patrol after getting lost and running out of fuel. Three of the five-man crew were killed:

Pilot Officer Edward Dudley Dear (82695)
Pilot Officer William Hotchkiss Edwards (81033)
Sergeant Stanley Donald Sutherland Goodlet (973901)

Their bodies were not recovered, though the remains of what was thought to be Goodlet were washed ashore a month later. The survivors, Sergeant Robert George Harkell and Pilot Officer David Arnold Eric Midgley, were interned in the Curragh.

On 11 March 1944 a Vickers Wellington XII HF311 from RAF 407 Squadron crashed into the sea near Clifden while attacking U-256. The pilot possibly misjudged the altitude when going in to attack. The crew of six were killed and only one body was recovered.

Pilot Officer Charles Grant J/18993 RCAF
Flight Officer Hugh Campbell Sorley J/20049 RCAF
Pilot Officer Franklin Leroy Travers J/90591 RCAF
Flight Officer Edmund Micheal O'Donnell J/16923 RCAF
Pilot Officer Reginald Carl Gaudet J/89118 RCAF
Pilot Officer Ivor Ernest Smithson J/89117 RCAF

Smithson's body was washed up in Derrygimbla, near Clifden, some months later and is buried there.

On 16 September 1944 an American PB4Y-1 Liberator from Norfolk, Virginia en route to Britain crashed near Ballyconnelly. Of the crew of ten, five died, while the survivors reached land at Aillebreack after being thirty-six hours afloat. The bodies were not recovered. They were as follows:

Ensign. Carl Grey Snavely Jr (co-pilot)
Ensign. Phillip Arthur Mills (navigator)
Airman Second Class Joseph Gerard Fleuchner (radio)
Airman Third Class Vernon Howard Petersen (mechanic)
Navy Seaman First Class Henry Elnathan Beckwith (gunner)

They are remembered on the Cambridge American Cemetery Tablets of the Missing and Buried at Sea. Beckwith died in the raft and his was the only body to be recovered. The survivors were brought back over the border. A bronze plaque telling their story was unveiled at Aillebrack by one of the survivors in 1994.

On 4 October 1944 a Vickers Wellington G.R. XIV HF450 from RAF 172 in Limavaddy went down in the bay near Salthill. Flight Officer David Gaudin of the RCAF drowned. The survivors were brought to the border. Gaudin's body was later washed ashore at Cnoc near Indreabhán and buried at Christchurch, Limavady.

An American war memorial at Aillebrack near Clifden.

INIS MÓR

> My legacy won't be riches. What I will leave is the sunshine to the flowers, honey to the bees, the moon above in the heavens for all those in love, and my beloved Aran Islands to the sea.
>
> BIGIT DIRRANE, AGED 108

There are twenty-seven nineteenth-century roadside memorials to the dead on Inis Mór, known as *leachta cuimhne*. There are also older ones further inland dating from the early 1700s at Cill Éinne. As with all cenotaphs, nobody is actually buried inside them. Unlike other cenotaphs in the county, these are square columns, measuring about 8 feet in height on one side and adorned with a simple stone cross. On the front is a cemented tablet asking for prayers for the soul of the deceased. They commemorate the families who lived and continue to live there such as the Fitzpatricks, McDonaghs, Dirranes, Wiggans, Mullens, Gills, O'Donnells, Naughtons, Conneelys, Hernons, and Folens. A lower plaque contains the names of those who erected it. Although the population was Gaelic-speaking, they are inscribed in English. The monuments were erected mostly before 1840 and commemorated peasants as opposed to landlords. It was believed that if the funeral procession halted a while to build a cairn it would stop the devil. Mairtín Ó Díreán made reference to the practice in '*Gáire na hEagla*', a poem about his brother's funeral in 1964. These monuments are only on Inis Mór.

The patron saint of Inis Mór is St Enda (†535), originally from Oriel, a kingdom in the north-east. He is buried at Teaghlach Éinne, a small church half-buried in the sand on the south-east of the island. The graveyard is still in use.

Overlooking Cill Éinne Bay, on the northern-shore side of the road at the village is *Leacht na nIascaire* (The Memorial to the Fishermen). It is a modern cenotaph built by the islanders in 1997 and dedicated to all who have drowned at sea. There are many names on it dating from the early nineteenth century. Each year on 15 August there is a memorial service at it for those who lost their lives at sea.

The nearby island of Inis Meáin houses the grave of St Kenderrig, a seventh-century princess from Leinster, behind the priest's house in the centre of the island. Every 15 August, the island women assemble there and at the well dedicated to the saint. The tradition is to circle the grave seven times and place a stone at the grave every time they pass by and then to drink from her well.

BEARNA

Bearna church has a tomb to the front of it that obviously predates the modern church built around 1975. It is the tomb of Marcus Lynch of Barna House, a man who owned over 4,000 acres of land. The tomb dates from 1857.

The bog at Bearna was used to 'disappear' people. Patrick Joyce was the principal of Bearna National School. His disappearance led to the reprisal murder of Father Griffin. On 16 October 1920, the IRA, having broken into the post office and intercepted letters from Patrick Joyce to Dublin Castle, came to his house and took him away. According to Geraldine Dillon, who gave a statement to the Bureau of Military History, a priest, Father Tom Burke, gave him the last rites, and when this was made known, the authorities suspected the priest was Father Griffin. Joyce had asked that his body be returned to his family, but this was denied. His wife and two sons moved to Dublin shortly after this. His relatives were never informed about the location of his body. The disappearance made national headlines but was soon forgotten about. It was only in July of 1998 that his remains were uncovered when a local amateur archaeologist came across them in the bog, not far from where the body of Father Griffin was dumped. A pocket watch and coins dating from the period were found with the remains. Joyce's three grandchildren, then in their late sixties and early seventies, returned to Galway to make the funeral arrangements. Another Joyce, the author of *Finnegan's Wake*, made reference to Patrick Joyce in the form of his character Persse O'Reilly, who consorted with the Black and Tans and was also shot as a spy.

The tomb of the Lynch family of Barna House.

Further west along the coast, close to Spidéal, somewhere in the landcape is the resting place of Roderic O'Flaherty or Ruaidhrí Ó Flaithbheartaigh (1629–1718?). He was born in Moycullen Castle and was the last lord of Iar Connacht, the domain of the O'Flahertys. He was also a noted historian, who documented much of the county's, as well as national, history and published two works, *Ogygia* and *A Chronographical Decription West of hIar Connacht*. He lost his lands in the Cromwellian confiscations and died in abject poverty.

FURBO

I arrived at the mausoleum at Furbo just before the rain swept in from the Atlantic. I had come to inspect the resting place of John Henry Blake adjacent to the church built in 1934, and obviously much older than it. I was surprised that it contained no inscription. The caretaker, Joe Hegarty, told me that efforts to restore the mausoleum proved too expensive and city funding was not forthcoming. Through a hole in the window the inside of the mausoleum can be viewed and the remains of rotten coffins and human bones can be seen.

John Henry Blake, born in 1808, was a land agent who was murdered on 29 June 1882. Land agents were usually Irish, belonging to the gentry, and often Catholic. He was the third and youngest son of Lieutenant-Colonel John Blake of Furbo, the first Catholic Mayor of Galway since the reign of James II when he served from 1830 to 1836, and Maria Galway of Cork. John Henry Blake worked first as a bailiff on the Blake estate at Furbo, but in the late 1830s moved to Kiltullagh, Athenry, to act as his infant nephew's land agent. He lived at Rathville House, Raford, in the parish of Kiltullagh and later became agent to Hubert de Burgh-Canning, 2nd Marquess of Clanricarde. Clanricarde was an absentee landlord, who lived in London, far removed from his tenants, and was widely believed to be the worst landlord in all of Ireland, infamous for evicting his tenants. He did not answer letters, and ignored petitions from the Bishop of Clonfert who wrote pleading for a reduction of rent owing to successive poor harvests, falling prices, and flooding. In January of 1881, he wrote to Blake showing contempt for them by stating: 'unless husbandmen can afford to plant something better than stones (or bad potatoes which are as useless as stones) they are not fit to be tenant farmers.'

The Blake mausoleum in Furbo.

It was Blake who would bear the brunt of the tenants' anger. Both he and his driver, Thady Ruane, were shot on the way to attend mass in Loughrea on 29 June 1882. His wife Harriet, who was present, survived the incident. Despite several months of investigation and seven arrests on suspicion, no one stood trial for the murders. His murder achieved nothing and he was replaced by Frank Joyce who carried on the evictions. While Blake was buried here, his wife Harriet, who died in 1917, was buried in Kiltullagh as were her sons Edmond (1876–1944) and Henry. Thady Ruane left thirteen children, most of whom emigrated. Although his grave is not marked, there is a large Ruane plot at Kiltullagh Cemetery.

INDREABHÁN

Directions: The graveyard is not easy to find. Take the L202 and once you cross a bridge take the first left, and after a series of twists and turns you eventually arrive down at the cemetery, which is located by the sea.

The presence of a large stone altar here suggests the local community celebrate mass on the beach. The cemetery suffered considerable damage during recent storms when it was ravaged by the Atlantic. Its wall has several boulders in place to protect it from the destruction of the powerful sea. There are two graveyards here, an old and a new one. The older one is somewhat uneven and few slabs have legible inscriptions, while many graves have been reclaimed by nature. Maybe having the earth embrace and envelop both the corpse and gravestone is the way things should be. The new graveyard has a grave commemorating three brothers who drowned tragically in Ceathrú Rua in 1984. It also holds the grave of Dr Noel Browne (1915-97) Browne was perhaps unique by virtue of having been a member of five different political parties. He co-founded the National Progressive Democrats and the Socialist Labour Party, was expelled from Fianna Fáil and resigned from both the Labour Party and Clann na Poblachta. As a government minister he controversially attended the requiem mass of the former President of Ireland, Douglas Hyde, in 1949. At the time, Catholics were forbidden from entering a Protestant

The grave of Doctor Noel Browne.

place of worship and the rest of the Catholic cabinet adhered to this and waited outside. His Waterloo was the Mother and Child Scheme. As part of the scheme, Browne proposed that the State would provide maternity care for all mothers and healthcare for children up to the age of 16. The Church's objections to it are well known, but medical doctors objected to it almost as strongly as they feared a loss of revenue. Nobody in the Dáil was willing to support him and in April of 1951, Seán MacBride, the party leader, demanded his resignation. The controversy caused the fall of the government with the Taoiseach, John A. Costello, leaving nobody in doubt as to the relationship between Church and State, infamously declaring in the Dáil: 'I, as a Catholic, obey my Church authorities and will continue to do so.'

Browne kept a low profile thereafter. His autobiography, *Against the Tide*, was published in 1986 and became a best seller. After retiring from Dáil Éireann, Browne moved to Baile na hAbhainn, County Galway with his wife Phyllis, where he died on 21 May 1997 at the age of 81. The inscription on the stone bench beside his grave describes him as a physician, politician and lifelong campaigner. His wife Phyllis is described as wife, political partner and soulmate.

Also in the Indreabhán area is a memorial, unveiled in June of 1970, to nine fishermen who lost their lives on 15 June 1917 when they found a barrel mine believed to be, but not necessarily so, German. It is unlikely they knew how deadly it was, and assuming it to be cargo from a sunken ship, towed it ashore to further examine it. One of the fishermen, Joe 'Hughie' Faherty, began to have doubts about the safety of the barrel and hid behind a rock. He would be the only survivor. The others removed a couple of screws from the head of the barrel, and then began to pull out a piece of chord. The blast was heard for miles around and little was found of the deceased. The men who died were:

Edward McDermott
Joseph Flaherty
Tim Keady
Peter Folan
Colm Feeney
Edward Lee
Manas Flaherty
Tom Hopkins
Peter Lee

CLIFDEN

> Death must be so beautiful. To lie in the soft brown earth, with the grasses waving above one's head, and listen to silence. To have no yesterday, and no tomorrow. To forget time, to forgive life, to be at peace.
>
> *THE CANTERVILLE GHOST*, OSCAR WILDE

Christchurch Anglican church, in the heart of Clifden and overlooking the town, was built in 1853, on the site of an older church, and has two graves of note. The churchyard holds the graves of Seán Lester (1888–1959) from Carrickfergus and the founder of Clifden, John D'Arcy (1785–1839). Lester was the last secretary-general of the League of Nations. He caused controversy when he was seconded as the League's representative to Danzig and irritated the Nazis by defending the Polish minority. He stood up to Hitler at a time when appeasement was the policy being pursued by countries such as France and Britain. Under pressure from Hitler, the League recalled him to Geneva. Though there were calls that he should stand for the

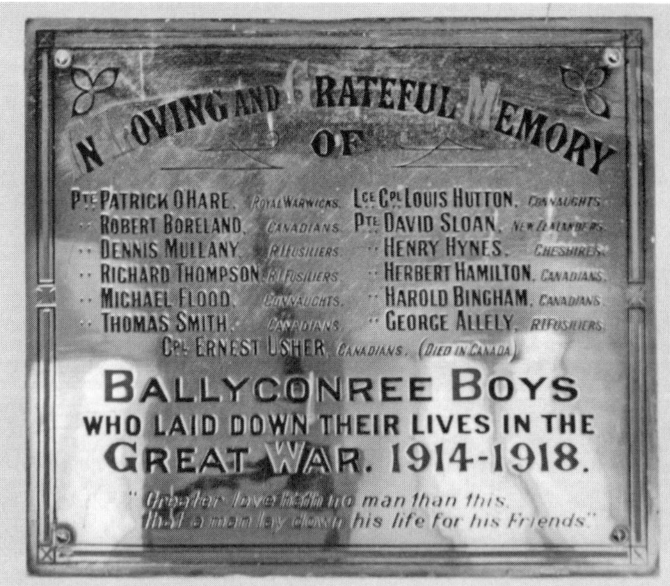

A First World War plaque in Christchurch, Clifden. Such plaques are seemingly exclusive to Church of Ireland churches. Where are the Catholics who fell in the conflict commemorated?

The tomb of John D'Arcy who founded Clifden.

An unsung hero of the thirties and last secretary-general of the League of Nations – Seán Lester.

Irish presidency, he retired from the limelight after the dissolution of the League and settled in Connemara. He is buried under a plain limestone slab, alongside his wife Elizabeth *née* Tyrrell (1897–1974) and their daughter Dorothy Mary Gageby (1922–2002).

John D'Arcy, who built Clifden Castle in 1815, wanted to have a commercial hub in an area which was poverty-stricken, and Clifden emerged as one of Ireland's newest towns after the construction of a pier, a road to Galway and a railway line. A monument to him overlooks the town. He produced fourteen children and there are several D'Arcy graves there but I could only establish which one was his with the help of some parishioners. The inscription is hardy legible. Inside the church itself it a brass plaque, commemorating the Ballyconree men who fell in the First World War. A variety of regiments are represented, including the Royal Irish Fusiliers and the Connaught Rangers. Some also seem to have fought in the Candian Army. The plaque bears the inscription 'greater love hath no man than this, that a man layeth his life down for his friends'.

BALLINAKILL

Directions: The picturesque St Thomas' church is located on a bend on the N59 between Letterfrack and Clifden.

The small Church of Ireland graveyard contains two war graves. The first one is that of Captain G.D. Morrow of the Canadian Artillery with the date 30 April 1941. The body of the 56-year-old captain from Winnipeg was washed ashore at Renvyle on 27 May 1941. He was a casualty of the SS *Nerissa*, which was sunk north-west of Ireland by U-552.

Another war grave is that of 19-year-old Ordinary Seaman J. Woodward (195393), who served on HMS *Mashona*. The *Mashona* was a Royal Navy destroyer that took part in the sinking of the *Bismarck* on 27 May 1941. She later came under heavy air attack from the Luftwaffe while returning to port the following day and sank off the coast of Galway with the loss of forty-eight men. Woodward's body was washed ashore. Under his serial number is the inscription 'He gave his all. Duty nobly done'.

The grave of Ordinary Seaman Woodward.

LETTERFRACK

What they suffered
They told but few
They did not deserve
What they went through
Tired and weary
They made no fuss
They tried so hard
To stay with us

WORDS INSCRIBED AT THE CEMETERY ENTRANCE IN LETTERFRACK

'If you don't behave you will be sent to Letterfrack' was a threat parents used in the 1970s to bring their misbehaving children into line, and children knew it to be a place for 'bold boys'. Letterfrack is a village about 84 kilometres from Galway city and infamous throughout the country for its industrial school. A wealthy English Quaker couple bought and developed a large parcel of land here in 1849 and wanted to build a school for the local children. In 1884, the property was sold to the Archbishop of Tuam, Dr John McEvilly, who petitioned the lord lieutenant of Ireland, Earl Spencer, for an industrial school there. The lord lieutenant was against the idea as he considered the location too remote and because there were no orphaned or wandering children in the area, but the archbishop got his way. It was not just delinquents who were sent there but also orphans and children from broken families. At its height in 1898, there were 8,000 children incarcerated in industrial schools on the island.

Although this was officially a school where education was supposed to take place, the bulk of the children's time was taken up with slave labour, working on the institution's farm, which made a profit. As its peak in 1950, Letterfrack had a 184 boys. It soon became notorious for its harsh regime, slave labour, beatings and sex abuse.

Those who escaped were brought back by the guards and local farmers. The locals believed it was an act of kindness as the ill-equipped boys would have died of exposure in the hills of Connemara. Food was as scarce as Christian love and the pupils were often undernourished and pale. The building was damp and the boys often had to work in wet clothes. In 1941, seven deaths were recorded. The cause of death was stated as consumption (tuberculosis) in five of these cases, and tuberculosis and pneumonia in the other two. Medical care in such a remote location would have been limited.

Some former inmates tried to draw attention to the abuses at Letterfrack, people such as Noah Kitterick, also known as Peter Tyrrell, who was an inmate there between 1924 and 1932. He campaigned to have the abusers brought to justice but was ignored by both Church and State, the former threatening to sue him for defamation. He was finally justified with the publication of the Ryan Report in 2009, but this came too late – tormented by Letterfrack and the lack of justice he set himself alight in London in 1967. The reform school finally closed in 1974.

The graveyard, hidden among the trees to the left of the local church, stands as a symbol to a hard-hearted society and the true horror sinks in after seeing how young many of the boys were. The most recent marked grave was from 1956. A single stone cross dating from 1968 records the names of sixty-one boys who died there. Along with the names is the brief inscription: 'Dear Lord grant eternal rest to all our deceased. You are all remembered by the brothers, lay staff and pupils of St Joseph's'. What was only discovered much later was that there were a lot more boys buried there in unmarked graves. In 2002, John Prior, who himself had been incarcerated in an industrial school in Tralee, began to clean up the overgrown cemetery. He also started doing research and discovered that seventy-seven boys were interred at Letterfrack. Further research revealed the figure was at least ninety-nine. There are seventy-seven marble-shaped hearts erected in 2002. It is not entirely clear how the boys died, though some doubtlessly succumbed to the influenza epidemic of 1918 and the TB epidemic of the 1950s. For some no death certificates were provided. Some of the black-marble hearts simply state 'died as a young boy', without any mention of their age. In the 1950s, some of the inmates were only 3 or 4 years' old and in the same area as teenagers.

The grave of Bernard Kerrigan which was only discovered in 2002.

Four-year-old Bernard Kerrigan died here in 1935 and was buried in an unmarked grave, which was soon forgotten. In 2002, a 74-year-old man turned up to the ceremony to commemorate the estimated ninety-nine boys buried there. He had played with Kerrigan as a child and was present at the burial. He had wanted to visit his grave before he died. The unmarked grave was eventually discovered and it posed awkward questions of why no record was kept of it. At the same ceremony in 2002, John Flanagan's brother was also present. Though seriously ill, he had made the journey from Dublin. His brother had died there on 28 January 1932 of pneumonia. There was no mention of him at the ceremony as there was no record of him, but his brother remembered where he was buried. Mannix Flynn, now an independent politician in Dublin, was one of the more famous inmates. He was sent there for stealing a box of chocolates and, on 22 December 2002, he gave an interview entitled 'To Hell in Connaught' to the *Irish Independent* describing what he experienced there. A poem, 'Lost Lives' by former pupil Desmond Philpott, who was incarcerated there in the 1960s, speaks volumes:

They took away our Childhood's
Our country's greatest shame

Abused and forgotten
Will never be the same.

No blame was ever taken
From those who put us there
Our cried went unnoticed
They left us in despair.

The memories of this past
Are sadly hard to bare [*sic*]
They never showed us love
And they didn't give a care.

MOYARD

And I shall have some peace there, for peace comes dropping slow.

WILLIAM BUTLER YEATS, 'THE LAKE ISLE OF INNISFREE'

Moyard is the final resting place of Oliver Joseph St John Gogarty (1878–1957), an Irish poet, author, doctor and senator. He was a contemporary of James Joyce and became the inspiration for Buck Mulligan in *Ulysses*. He was surgeon to Arthur Griffin and dressed the body of Michael Collins for his funeral. As a Free State senator he became a target for the IRA, who kidnapped him and planned to murder him, but he managed to escape and swam the Liffey to safety. His time in the senate was controversial. On the issue of birth control he remarked, 'I think it is high time the men of this country found some other way of loving God than by hating women'. He was also against the revival of the Irish language, proposing that the funding be used instead for housing, education and health services. The senate was dissolved by De Valera in 1936. Gogarty brought out several books of poetry which his friend W.B. Yeats was eager to promote. Yeats might have over-estimated Gogarty's abilities when he referred to him in his *Oxford Book of Modern Verse* (1936) as to 'one of the great lyric poets of our age'.

The grave of Oliver St John Gogarty at Moyard.

Gogarty went to live in America, and believing he was too old to practice medicine, tried to live off his poetry. He collapsed and died on the street in New York in 1957. His remains were flown home and buried at Moyard Cemetery overlooking the sea. He is buried with his wife Martha Mary Dunne who died a year later. The ashes of his son, Oliver Duane Gogarty (1907–99), were scattered over the grave when he passed away. The inscription on the grave slab, which is at a 45-degree angle, reads:

Our friends go with us as we go
Down the long path where beauty winds
Where all Love forgathers
Why should we fear to join our friends?
Non dolet

CLEGGAN

Over the rocks and the waves high,
Out on the cliffs the sea-birds cry.
The night wears through and dawn is night.
And I am still alone, alone,
My man is gone, he is young to die,
And I am left alone, mavrone.

A CLEGGAN WOMAN'S LAMENT

The Cleggan Bay Disaster of 1927 devastated a community reliant on the sea for survival. Cleggan is a small village 10 kilometres north-west of Clifden. It was a calm but cold October evening in the middle of herring season when the fishermen set out. There were no signs of the storm that was about to approach. The first indication of the winds came from a roaring sea from the far side of Inisboffin and no matter how able the fishermen considered themselves, they knew their only chance of survival was to head for shore. As the men rowed

The Cleggan Bay Disaster monument at Lackagh.

towards shore contending with gusts of 70 miles an hour, some of the boats capsized. Sixteen men from Rossadillisk died in Cleggan Bay shortly after 7 pm that October evening. Nine men from Inisboffin also perished. It is believed many of those who drowned did so while trying to save their precious nets. There were twenty houses in the village of Rossadilisk. More than half had been affected by the tragedy. The victims are buried in the churchyard of Omey, a peninsula with the sea nearly on all sides. A plaque in Lacken commemorates them, and there is also a monument to them on Omey Island.

KYLEMORE

Directions: Kylemore Abbey is one of the tourist highlights of Connemara. Take the N59 towards Clifden. Turn right after Recess and go through the Inagh Valley, taking a left when you come to the junction.

The castle was built by Mitchell Henry (1826–1910) for his wife Margaret (1829–1874) *née* Vaughan of Quilly House, County Down. They had honeymooned in the area and fallen in love with it. Henry, a

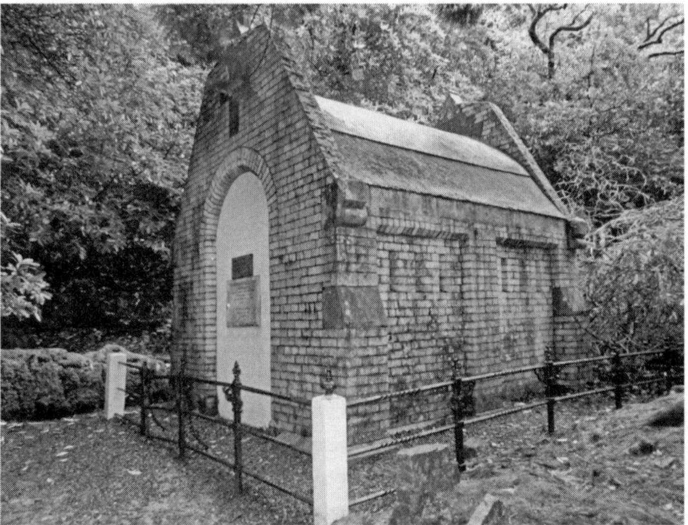

The Henry mausoleum at Kylemore.

Manchester merchant of Irish parentage, would represent Galway as an MP between 1871 and 1885, becoming the first home-ruler to represent Galway. He built Kylemore between 1863 and 1868. A portrait of Margaret Henry is on display in the castle. She died of dysentery while on holiday in Egypt four years after the castle's completion. Her husband had her body embalmed and brought back to Kylemore. When Mitchell Henry died in England he was cremated and his ashes were brought to Kylemore, so he could be beside his beloved wife. The remains of John Henry, a grandnephew of Mitchell Henry who died on 13 February 1989, were also laid to rest in the mausoleum. The inscription reads: 'Margaret beloved wife of Mitchell Henry of Kylmore Castle. Died Dec 4 in Cairo 1874 aged 45. Mitchell Henry died Nov 22 1910 aged 85'.

Henry also had a church, a miniature replica of Bristol Cathedral, built in memory of his wife, which is open to the public. Beside the church are the graves of the Benedictine nuns, some of whom came over from Ypres when their convent was destroyed in the First World War. They acquired the property and it became a boarding school for girls until its closure in 2010.

OUGHTERARD

Síleann do chara agus do namhaid nach bhfaighidh tú bás choíche.

Your friend and your enemy think you will never die.

SEANFHOCAL/PROVERB

Directions: Kilcummin Cemetery is just before the village on the right-hand side as you approach from Galway.

The older section of the graveyard is overgrown and greatly neglected. One of the most famous visitors to this cemetery was James Joyce. Joyce listened to Nora Barnacle's tales of her life in Galway and weaved them into his work. He got his wires crossed, and thought that a former boyfriend of hers was from Oughterard, which is why Furey in 'The Dead' comes from here.

A granite stone bears the inscription 'Colm de Bhailís 1796–1906 file agus Fear ceirde'. He was an Irish poet and songwriter from Garumna. He trained as a stonemason and travelled extensively throughout the country. His work seems to have been very popular in the nineteenth century. A picture of him was taken in 1903 when he was 107. While in the poorhouse, a local man, Pádraig Ó Domhnalláin (1884–1960) wrote down his songs and Conradh na Gaeilge published a collection of his work in 1904. Patrick Pearse had his work published in *An Claidheamh Soluis*, and though de Bhailís received a fee for this, it was not enough and he died at Oughterard Poorhouse in 1906.

I was in two minds whether or not I should write about David Smith. The local Galway newspapers did not comment on his existence in Galway, nor indeed of his passing in 2012, and I only knew he was in Galway from reading American and British newspapers. His is an unassuming name, but it is instantly recognisable when connected to the infamous Moors murders. Galway has long had the reputation of a place where you could retire from the limelight and people would leave you alone. This is perhaps one reason why David Smith, brother-in-law of Myra Hindley, chose to live here. When 17-year-old

The grave of Colm de Bhailís.

David Smith and his then-wife, Maureen, phoned the Manchester Police in 1965, they put a stop to a series of horrific murders known as the Moors Murders. The call saved the lives of other innocent children, but David's participation was never acknowledged. Quite the opposite: Hindley and Brady tried to implicate him in the murders and many believed them to the extent that life in England became unbearable for him. Hindley, who died in 2002, only retracted his accusations in 1987, and Smith was assaulted on a regular basis and had his property destroyed. After his marriage to Maureen, who died

The Republican plot at Oughterard.

of a brain haemorrhage in 1980, ended in divorce, Smith married a Connemara woman. Shortly before his death, Smith wrote a book, *Evil Relations* (2012), detailing that fateful night when he witnessed 17-year-old Edward Evans being axed to death by the deranged Brady. The grave has a passage from the book, which encouraged me to write about him, and by highlighting his case I hope that his contribution to humanity will someday be recognised.

The graveyard also has a Republican plot easily recognisable by the tricolour. It was here that the anti-treaty IRA man Séamus Ó Máille (1897–1923) was buried. Along with five others, he was taken from Galway Jail and executed by Free State troops in the Old Workhouse in Tuam on 11 April 1923. They had been found guilty of having rifles and ammunition. They were buried within the workhouse and when the Free State Army vacated it at the end of the year, despite pleas from relatives to return the bodies to the families, they were reinterred Athlone Barracks. The families did not give up and in October the following year the bodies were finally returned to them. Also interred in the plot is Seán MacGabhain, who died in 1925 of wounds received during the Civil War.

ROSCAHILL

> In the midst of life we are in death. Earth to earth, ashes to ashes, dust to dust; in sure and certain hope of the Resurrection into eternal life.
>
> BOOK OF COMMON PRAYER, 'THE BURIAL OF THE DEAD' (1662)

Directions: Follow the N59. Take the second turn right after Moycullen, then the first right after the Church of Killannin.

Killannin was named after St Annin, a female recluse. Sir William Wilde, cataloguing the monuments along the banks of the Corrib, made reference to the site in 1867, saying it was 'romantically situated among massive rocks and boulders, in the midst of an ancient and well-filled graveyard'. The old burial ground at Killannin is the final resting place of Major Poppleton (1775–1827), orderly officer and friend of

The Martin family tomb, containing the remains of Major Poppleton.

Napoleon when he was in exile on St Helena. The tomb is easy to find and belongs to the Martins, the local landlords who gained control of the area after the O'Flahertys were dispossessed in the seventeenth century. Poppleton spent two years with the former emperor and on their parting was presented with a silver snuff box. It has been claimed that the tomb itself is in the shape of a snuff box, but there are several tombs in this shape in the county. He was later stationed in Galway, where, at a military ball, he met his future wife Margaret, daughter of Nicholas Martin of Ross. Much of the inscription on the tomb is no longer legible but I could make out the following: 'Here lies the body of Major Thomas William Poppleton of the 53rd Regiment, a brave and accomplished Christian soldier, he was honoured by the esteem of the Emperor Napoleon. Died October 1827'.

On the same tomb is reference to Richard James Martin of the King's Dragoon Guards who died in 1854 but does not appear to have been a casualty of the Crimean War. The tomb was vandalised at some stage and through the crack it is possible to see that it goes down at least 10 feet below the surface. The tomb contains a great deal of inscription, which is sadly fading away.

Beside the old ruined church is a mortuary chapel, where the Martins were also interred. The chapel has no roof and is exposed to the elements. The copperplate inscription, in a state of good preservation, reads as follows:

> Here lieth the body of Anton Martin Fiz Richard of Dangan. Esteemed in life, dutieus son, the tender husband, the truly affectionate, faith steady in friendship, frugal human, temperate valiant beneficent to the distressed. Only to punish in gratitude and impiety. He parted this life the 13 of May 1748 in the sixty fourth year of life.

The entrance to the vault is open and when I descended the steps all I could see was rubble so I did not investigate any further. An iron gate lies beside the entrance with the inscription 'Archer Martin 1888'. He was living in Ontario at the time, his grandfather having emigrated in 1833. He returned on a visit in 1888 and paid for gates at the graveyard entrance and the family mort house.

The Martin family mortuary chapel.

7

NORTH GALWAY

Is feoite caite 'tá na blátha scaipead ar do leaba chaoilse;
ba bhreá iad tamall ach thréig a dtaitneamh, níl snas ná brí iontu.
'S tá an bláth ba ghile liom dár dhás ar ithir riamh ná a fhásfaidh choíche
ag dreo sa talamh, is go deo ní thacfaidh ag cur éirí croí orm.

Spent and withered are the flowers scattered
on your narrow bed.
They were fair a while but their brightness faded,
they've no gloss or life.
And my brightest flower that in the soil ever
or will ever grow
Rots in the ground, and will come no more
to lift my heart.

PÁDRAIG Ó HÉIGEARTAIGH, 'OCHÓN! A DHONNCHA'

ANNAGHDOWN

On 4 September 1828 a boat called *An Caisleán Nua* left the pier at Annaghdown to go to a fair in Galway. There were thirty-one people on board, all from the Annaghdown area, as well as some sheep that were to be sold at the fair. Tragedy struck as they approached Menlo. It was an old boat, belonging to Tomás Ó Fearaíl, and when a sheep put its hoof through the bottom, one of the men tried to plug the hole with his coat. By doing so, he pushed out the rotten plank and water flowed in. Nineteen people died in what was one of the worst drowning tragedies in Irish history. Some of them, such as John Cosgrave, could swim, but were drowned as desperate people clung to them. The bodies were brought ashore near Menlo Castle. The disaster would have been forgotten were it not for the famous poem composed by Raftery. Raftery's poem, meant to be sung, was a way of spreading the news and recalling the history of a suppressed people. In 1978, divers discovered what they believed to be the remains of the boat about 100 yards upstream from Menlo Pier. Nobody from Annaghdown could tell me where the victims' graves are and their mortal remains have long since faded into the landscape.

A monument to those who died in the Annaghdown tragedy.

ROSS ERRILLY

Located close to Headford and in some accounts referred to as the Abbey of Ross, Ross Errilly is considered the best-preserved Francisan friary in the country. It was founded on a narrow strip of land surrounded by marshland accessed by a narrow causeway, with the help of Raymond de Burgo in 1351 and Archbishop McHugh. At the time, the plague was ravaging the countryside and the archbishop was guided in a vision to the spot where he was to build the friary. He himself died of the plague shortly after its completion. It suffered considerably in Elizabethan and Cromwellian times as well as from the upheaval which was followed with the penal laws. It was abandoned by 1830 and fell into decay.

The graves of Ross Errilly read like a who's who in the area. Many of the grave plaques are legible and the oldest I could find was from 1646. Names of the tribes such as Bodkin and Lynch as well as Burke are omnipresent here. Though it is no longer marked, this is the final resting place of Brian Oge O'Rourke (†1604), the last king of

The Lynch mausoleum at Ross Errilly.

The coat of arms of Ulick Burke at Ross Errilly.

Breifne. After hearing of his father's execution in London, he sided with Red Hugh O'Donnell and fought the English at the Battle of Curlew Pass. It was from Ross Errilly that the O'Donnells of Donegal invited monks to set up an abbey in Donegal town in 1474. A mausoleum of the Lynch family is also on site. The inscription reads: 'This tomb was erected by Charles Joseph Lynch of Petersburg House Co. Mayo. He died 1863 aged 49 years of age.'

In his book *From the Saxon in Ireland, or the Rambles of an Englishman in Search of a Settlement in the West of Ireland*, John Harvey Ashworth described Ross Errilly in 1851 as being devoid of both humans and animals. He was perturbed to find sixty skulls lying around on the ground. Another visitor, Revd Otway, who visited the site in 1839, was less perturbed and wrote in *A Tour in Connaught* that he removed a moss-covered skull as souvenir. The noted archaeologist Sir William Wilde visited the ruins in July 1866 and also wrote about heaps of skulls and bones. The site had a reputation for unburied human remains being desecrated by cattle and sheep. This was not unusual in Irish churchyards in general. In other parts of the country, such as at Rathmichael in the Dublin Mountains, there were 'skull holes', pits used to store bones taken out of graves when space was an issue.

KILLURSA

Killursa is about 1½ miles west of Headford on the Greenfields Road. The name comes from *cill*, meaning the small church, of Fursa, the saint who built the church there back in the sixth century, though the ruin there now dates from around the thirteenth century. Another monument worth noting in the graveyard is a cenotaph dating from 1673. These kinds of cenotaphs are common in the Galway area especially on Inis Mór. The inscription is partially obscured by lichens, but it seems to be dedicated to a cleric and states: 'Pray for the soul of Father John _______ who died in his 40th year of age on the 20th day of March in the year of our Lord 1767'.

On the other side, the plaque has a chalice symbol, the letters 'IHS' and the name of another cleric who died in 1763.

A cenotaph at Killursa.

DONAGHPATRICK

All that live must die, passing through nature to eternity.

WILLIAM SHAKESPEARE

The graveyard at Donagh Patrick, from the Irish *Domhnach Phádraig* meaning 'the sanctuary of St Patrick', is well known for its Republican plot. As the Civil War progressed it was decreed that anyone found in possession of a weapon would be tried by a military court, a court that usually passed a death sentence. On 20 January 1923, five anti-Treaty IRA men were shot by firing squad in Custume Barracks, Athlone. There was much foot-dragging before the bodies were released to the relatives several months later. Four of the men were from Galway and were interred in the Republican plot at Donaghpatrick.

Michael Walsh, Derrymore
Herbert Collins, Kickeen, Headford
Stephen Joyce, Derrymore, Caherlistrane
Martin Burke, Caherlistrane

The tomb of Eva O'Flaherty.

Also interred here were the Tuam martyrs (see p.151).

The tomb of Mary Roche, who died in 1871, has a Celtic cross mounted on it, two memorials in one, and is unique in this regard. The Celtic cross appears to have been added by a son living in Philadelphia. In a corner of the graveyard is the well-maintained tomb of Eva O'Flaherty (1874–1963). She was born to the wealthy

The Republican plot at Donaghpatrick.

surroundings of Lisdonagh House, Caherlistrane and was educated in Dublin. She joined Cumann na mBan and became friends with most of the revolutionaries of the time. In 1910, she moved to Achill and founded St Colman's Knitting Industries, which became a major employer for the local women and lasted until 1970. Together with Darrell Figgis, the man who wrote the Irish Constitution, she founded Scoil Acla, Ireland's longest-running summer school. She died in Tuam and her biography, *Achill's Eva O'Flaherty – Forgotten Island Heroine*, was written by Mary J. Murphy.

TUAM

Tuam made international headlines a few years ago when it became public that the remains of nearly 800 babies had been found in what was believed to be a septic tank on the site of the former Mother and Baby Home. Up until the mid-twentieth century, single mothers were forced into such homes to hide their 'shame', and though they could look after their babies until they reached the age of 2, they were often forced to give them up for adoption after that. The site of the former home is well hidden within a housing estate. The casual visitor will not stumble across it by chance. Even today, nobody knows for sure who was buried there. It is a contentious issue in the town. Athough the remains made international headlines, local media kept its reporting low-key or wrote about it as if it were somewhere far removed from Galway. For this reason, I consulted British newspapers for information. Local historian Catherine Corless had 'discovered' the remains, which had been an open secret in Tuam for decades. She started her research with the nuns, the Bon Secours Sisters, who ran the home, but while wishing her well in her research they declined to assist her. When the news made world headlines, however, they became more cooperative and she was invited to meet them in a hotel in Galway, where they offered to make a donation to the collection for a memorial plaque. They did, however, question her findings, and argued that some of the bodies belonged to famine victims. The nuns were not the only ones to be disinterested. In an interview with *The Guardian*, Corless said:

'I couldn't understand it. We were shocked. We expected an outrage. The only ones who were outraged seemed to be us. The mentality seemed to be: "That's a long time ago, forget about it, it doesn't matter any more."'

She searched records at nearby cemeteries and found no names that matched up with the list of children's deaths given to her by the Births, Marriages and Deaths Registry. What shocks outsiders is that everyone in Tuam knew they were there but did not want to know about them. Catherine Corless said:

> The nuns left it as a wilderness. It was only when the locals found that there were bones there that they took it upon themselves to mind that graveyard for the past 40 years. It is credit to them – not to the town council, not to the county council, not to the church – just a few locals who had a heart and said, 'This is not right'.

The children from the home were treated differently, and though they attended the same schools as the local children, the latter were instructed to shun them. While some of the children died of measles or the whooping cough, others died from less-serious complaints such as laryngitis or abscesses, which many believe indicated neglect. Corless demanded answers and sought to have a plaque with the names of the deceased erected, to afford the deceased the dignity denied them in this life. As with the Magdalene graves in Galway, this was met with opposition. A small plaque was erected, but with no names. It simply states: 'In loving memory of those buried here. Rest in peace.' At the time of writing this, it is lamentable to report that the matter has yet to be resolved and has been swept under the carpet.

Right beside the unmarked mass grave is another bitter memory. On Wednesday 11 April 1923, the same day IRA leader Liam Lynch was shot, six men were taken from Galway Jail and shot on the grounds of the workhouse in Tuam, which was occupied by the Free State Army at the time. They had been arrested with arms and ammunition and sentenced to death. At the time, the Free State, in an effort to stop the war, was executing anyone caught with a firearm. The wall where

The infamous unmarked graveyard on the site of Tuam's Mother and Baby Home. Note the small plaque on the right, the only acknowledgement that people are buried here.

they were shot was to be demolished but was saved following protests from Tuam Sinn Féin. It stands as an ugly reminder to a brutal beginning of a new country. A month later the Civil War came to an end. The men who were shot that morning were:

Francis Cunnane, John Newell and Michael Monaghan
from Headford.
John McGuire from Cross Cong
Martin Moylan from Annaghdown
James O'Malley from Oughterard

All were buried in the Republican plot at Caherlistrane, save O'Malley (Ó Máille) who is interred in his native place (see p.139).

TEMPLE JARLATH

Temple Jarlath, dating from around 1360 and named after the founder of Tuam, is the oldest graveyard in the town. St Jarlath, who lived in the sixth century, was told by St Brendan to set up a church where his cartwheel broke. The age of the graveyard is uncertain, though recent excavations uncovered skeletal remains that could be dated back to the early eighth century, and it was used for burial until the new cemetery opened in 1884. As a sign of the times we live in, the cemetery has to be locked up to prevent anti-social behaviour, but the key can be obtained locally.

Some of the gravestones reveal the occupation of the deceased: a compass, the sign of a mason, appears on one, a plough stands for a farmer while for shepherds the symbols are shears and crook. According to local lore, the Fenians used some of the tombs to hide weapons. One of the tombs was known as the 'tomb of the floating coffin'. Unfortunately, I could not find any local who knew the meaning behind this.

In the tower of the chapel, guarded by an iron gate, is an Egan grave erected by Patrick Egan to his wife Eliza, who died on 20 June 1835 at the age of 32. The wall plaque in copperplate writing on the wall behind the grave slab, entitled 'the last request', reads as follows:

Effigy of lovers parting at death, Temple Jarlath.

Wilt thou?
I know thou wilt, sad silence speaks assent
And in the pleasing hope Eliza lies content
Here by words can be expressed
The mind of man when broken hearted
For sighs or tears console the breast
From all it loves ever parted
Then every grief I have to tell
In one sad solemn word – farewell

Above this dedication is a vandalised image of a man seated by his wife's bedside, watching in desperation as she departs from this life.

TUAM CEMETERY

The Victorian Tuam Cemetery is located on the Athenry Road and dates from the same time as New Cemetery in Galway. As you go in the main entrance to the right is the grave of Michael Moran (1893–1921) who, according to the inscription, died for his country at the age of 29. A native of Carramoneen, he was arrested in November 1920 and 'shot while escaping' from the RIC at Nun's Island in Galway city. According to the witness statement of Thomas Wilson, Old IRA, he was the battalion officer in command of the local IRA who launched an attack on Barnadearg RIC Barracks on Easter Saturday night 1920, and was involved in the Gallagh Ambush in which two RIC men were shot dead. About 200 unarmed IRA Volunteers marched at his funeral. When the British military saw they were marching in formation, they disrupted the cortège. The RIC were absent from the funeral. Also in the graveyard is a Connaught Rangers grave, that of Private S. Holian (3/3968) who fell on 24 June 1915.

Tuam has long associations with the travelling community and there are several traveller graves in the cemetery. They tend to stand out as being bigger, more personal and ornate. While they have attracted negative attention in recent years, in years gone by it was not uncommon for their graves to be unmarked, as a plaque on the wall reminds the visitor. It is customary for the traveller community to assemble at the grave when the headstone is unveiled, a year after the funeral: this is known as the blessing of the headstone. I spoke to Martin Collins, director of Pavee Point, about traveller funerals, which tend to be more informal than those of the settled community. In times gone by, it was customary to burn the caravan of the deceased along with their personal items. This was a custom that may have had its origins among Hindus, and was also a practical way of stopping the spread of disease. This practice ceased in the 1980s when trailers became more expensive and travellers started to move into houses. Eulogies are uncommon; songs at a funeral are usual and typically a man walks alongside the hearse as it leaves the church, singing, while the mourners follow behind in absolute silence. The corpse is seldom waked at home, and travellers prefer not to die at home. Funerals are a huge event and travellers will come from all over the country to attend.

A plaque to travellers interred in Tuam Cemetery.

LAVALLY

Lavally is located between Tuam and Clonbern. Just before the church at Lavally is a large stone reminding the visitor of the existence of a caltra or cemetery for unbaptised children. Beside it is a monument from the Second World War to commemorate seven Allied airmen based in Rufforth, Yorkshire flying a Halifax EB 134, who lost their lives when the bomber crashed into Ryehill ringfort on 7 November 1943. Only two of the crew wore dog tags. The others were identified by personal items such as letters and pictures. The bodies were taken over the border to RAF Aldergrove, Antrim. They were on training flight to practise fighter interception and went off course. The plane crashed at midnight, possibly after running out of fuel. The monument, complete with a small metal model of the bomber, was erected in 2007 by the local people. The following is a list of the crew, where they were from and where they are interred:

The Lavally monument in memory of seven Allied airmen who lost their lives here in 1943.

Pilot Sergeant Allan Stewart Johnston RAAF from Victoria
(Irvinestown Church of Ireland Cemetery)

Sergeant Robert Mair Clark RAF from Lanarkshire
(Danzil Airbles Cemetery, Motherwell)

Sergeant Edgar W. Camp RAF from Plymstock
(St Mary's and All Saints' Churchyard, Devon)

Flight Lieutenant Anthony J. Gallagher RAAF from Victoria
(Irvinestown Catholic Cemetery)

Flight Lieutenant George Hilton Sansome RAAF from Australia
(Irvinestown Church of Ireland)

Sergeant Leslie H. Wildman RAF from London
(Chingford Mount Cemetery, Essex)

Warrant Officer Norman W. Gardner RCAF Ontario
(Irvinestown Church of Ireland)

KNOCKMAA

Knockmaa is located just off the N17 towards Caherlistrane and is well signposted. The hill has strong mythological connections and was used for burial from ancient times. Some believed this provided it with divine protection. Michael Dames, author of *Mythic Ireland*, believed it was a site for cult practices as important as Uisneach or Cruachan. The first woman to come to Ireland was Cessair, granddaughter of Noah, who according to the eleventh-century *Lebor Gabhála* (Book of Invasions), landed forty days after the Great Flood. At the summit of the hill is a cairn or heap of rocks known as Carn Ceasra, said to be her final resting place. Knockmaa was also believed to be where Finnbheara, king of the Connacht faerie, held court. A plain stone cross on the summit marks the grave of Lieutenant General Sir Denis Kirwan Bernard, last member of the Kirwans of Castlehackett. He was not very popular in the area. As an RIC man, he fought the IRA in County Cork during the War of Independence. The local IRA burnt his house down in 1923, destroying priceless treasures in the process, when they feared the Free Staters would use the house. His home was rebuilt by some of those who burnt it down and he always feared it would be burnt down again.

He continued with his military career and rose to become a brigadier-general and colonel-in-chief of the Royal Ulster Rifles between 1937 and 1947. He also served as governor in Bermuda between 1939 and 1940. He died in 1956 and left no children. It is said that he was buried in an upright position so that he could look over his estate. It took five days for the estate workers to dig the grave and it was dug, some believe deliberately, on the wrong side on the estate boundary so that he was buried on his neighbour's land.

DUNMORE

Is iomaí lá sa chill orainn.	We owe the grave many a day.

SEANFHOCAL/PROVERB

The small town of Dunmore, about 10 miles outside Tuam on the N83, has three burial grounds worth noting. On 20 May 1921 three unidentified men took chemist Thomas McKeever from his boarding house and murdered him. He was found with a sign stating that the IRA had shot him as an informer. According to local IRA man, Thomas Mannion, who gave a witness statement to the Bureau of Military History in 1956, McKeever was not a spy. Nor does he appear to have been in the IRA, and Matt Doyle of the National Graves Association told me he is not on their roll of honour. A certain amount of mystery surrounds his murder. At a mass said for McKeever, the local priest, Dean McKenna, accused the Crown forces of murder. McKeever was not from the parish and is believed to be interred in his native Cork. A plaque was erected in his memory at the spot near the castle on Clooneen Bridge where his body was found.

Dunmore and East Galway in general were known for their pipers, and the piper Reilly, who lived there since 1864, was one of the most famous ones. Just as you enter the village of Dunmore across from the church is a monument to him, erected by Comhaltas Ceoltóirí Éireann in 1977 extolling his abilities as a piper. Local historian Hubert Birmingham told me that though his funeral in 1929 was a grand affair, the location of his grave in the new cemetery, just before the village on the Galway side, is unknown.

THE OLD DUNMORE GRAVEYARD

Here lies one whose name was writ in water.

EPITAPH OF JOHN KEATS

The graveyard is believed to be late-medieval. There used to be an old church beside the graveyard, but this was demolished several decades ago in the name of progress. The graveyard contains an unusual gravestone from 1858, encased in iron, the only one of its kind I came across in the county. Many of the older, large grave slabs have been placed close together. This may be a spacial issue but it could also be an effort to deter grave robbers. In many graveyards, the body was removed by digging a tunnel a few yards away and burrowing down at an angle. A child or suitably small person would be sent down, break open the coffin and pull out the corpse. All this could be done without any signs that the plot had been interfered with. This is well illustrated in Glasnevin Museum.

I first visited the graveyard in the 1990s and it was overgrown to the extent that very few of the graves could be inspected. The bushes and brambles have since been cut back and monuments such as Peter Delaney's have been revealed for the first time in decades. Peter Delaney was president of Galway GAA, albeit its shortest on record, dying in office after only a few days, and an Irish nationalist. The inscription reads:

> In memory of Peter Delaney Irish Patriot who died March 9 1895 Aged 35 Years. In recognition of his many noble qualities particularly his unflinching devotion to the sacred cause of Irish liberty. This monument has been erected by his comrades who will strive to make their native land a nation once again. God save Ireland.

The grave of
Peter Delaney.

A lack of space or a deterrent for grave robbers?

A fund of £30 was collected from representatives of different counties for the monument.

Although the grave can no longer be found, this cemetery is the final resting place of bard Cormac Dall Ó Comáin, who was born in 1703 at Wooodstock, near Ballindangan, County Mayo. Like Raftery, he became blind from smallpox at a very early age and learnt how to play the fiddle so he could support himself in later life. He had a talent for poetry, genealogy, history and legends and his recitals made him a popular figure at weddings and gatherings. One of his works that survived was the 'Lament for John Burke of Carrentryle', dedicated to the man who owned the Carantryla estate before the

A rare gravestone encased in iron in Dunmore Old Graveyard, the only example I came across in the entire county.

Handcocks in 1753. He died in Dunmore in 1790 and was buried here. The old graveyard closed in 1909 when the new graveyard, just before the town, was opened.

DUNMORE FRIARY

Just off the main square is the Augustinian Friary founded by Walter de Birmingham in 1425. A burial ground was situated outside its walls, and was demolished in the eighteenth century to make way for the road. When pipes were being laid in the street in 2006, 288 human remains were uncovered. The discovery of gunmoney dated them to the Williamite War of the late-seventeenth century. Gunmoney was scrap metal used as token currency in the Jacobite Army until the defeat in 1691. One of the skeletons had a nail hammered into the back of its head, suggesting an execution. The remains had been disturbed when the road itself was built in the eighteenth century, and it

A gravestone at Dunmore friary with raised lettering and very little space between the words. It reads 'Miss Barbara Burke dyed December the 10th. 1729'.

The tomb of the Handcocks.

is believed that Lord Ross, for whom the road was built, had the grave markers removed. The friary is the resting place of the Handcocks, the owners of Carantryla House. The last owner was Major Gerald Carlisle Handcock (1858–1938), who fought in the Sudan and Boer wars. His niece, Evelyn Handcock Ferguson, who died in 1988, decades after the house was demolished, is also interred here.

CARANTRYLA

Located about 5 kilometres outside the town, just off the Dublin Road, is the area of Carantryla. The place has fascinated me for years as my late grandmother was born in the Big House there and I wrote about it in *Fadó Fadó More Tales of Lesser-Known Irish History*. It vanished from the landscape in the post-colonial orgy of official destruction. Though the big house is gone, a crypt remains, located in a ringfort known as the House Fort. For reasons best known to the perpetrators, the monument was vandalised at some stage. The steps leading into it were blocked with stones to prevent further desecration and, according to

The grave of the Handcock sisters, cruelly treated by their own mother. In the foreground are the blocked steps leading into the crypt.

Patrick Hessian, who currently owns the land and was kind enough to show me around, it contains three lead coffins. Landlords were respected and often feared. When their power was taken away, bitterness came to the fore and many saw anything connected to this time as something that should be destroyed. The panel on the grave is only partially legible. The inscription that can be deciphered reads: 'Here planted in memory of the amiably and lamented owner of Carantryla Mrs Anne Handcock who died August 1818 aged 35'.

Also interred there are three Handcock sisters: Josephine, Anne Mary and Honoria. Nobody knows for sure how they died, but many locals claim that they were poisoned by their own mother, Catherine *née* Kelly, who wanted the estate for her son John Delacour, whose father was Ulick John de Burgh, the Earl of Clanricarde (1802–74) of Portumna. The Handcock divorce and settlement made considerable headlines at the time and were the source of much amusement in *The New York Times* as Clanricarde tried to deny, even in the face of strong evidence, that he was the father of Delacour. While the mother might not have been totally blameless in their demise, it is more likely that the girls died from TB.

My grandmother lived in Killoney and told me of an old grave there. A cholera epidemic struck Dunmore long before the Great Famine of 1847. It was believed that the disease was brought there by a man who had worked on the docks in Liverpool. The neighbours suspected that a mother and son were dead but were afraid to approach the house as the disease was highly contagious. One man was, however, brave enough to investigate. He made a shroud and carried them off towards the graveyard. However, the route to the graveyard would have meant going through the town, and people did not want that in case they caught the disease, so he buried them in Tully's field in Páirc Mhór. Years later it is believed that a relative came home from America and had the tomb erected over their graves, which is still there, guarded by a lone hawthorn tree. The inscription is no longer legible, but local historian Jim Greaney, who wrote a history of the parish in the 1980s, describes it as: 'O Lord have mercy on the souls of Maggie Brehony and her son Tom who died on 25th September 1765, aged 63 and 31 years'.

A lonely tomb guarded by a lone hawthorn.

GLENAMADDY

Glenamaddy has two monuments connected to the RIC, one revered, the other long-forgotten. Just off the main square is a plaque to Jeremiah Mee who led the Listowel mutiny and is buried in Glasnevin. The grave of District Inspector Peter Burke (62175) is in the local cemetery. He was shot dead in a pub in Balbriggan on 20 September 1920.

The forgotten grave of Peter Burke, whose assassination was the catalyst for the Sacking of Balbriggan.

He was celebrating his promotion with his brother Michael, who was also in the RIC, when the IRA entered the premises and a gun battle ensued. According to Richard Abbott, the IRA used dum dum bullets that exploded upon impact. Peter was killed outright and Michael seriously injured. The Auxiliaries went on a rampage when they heard the news, which lead to a number of premises being destroyed and the deaths of two people. The incident became known as 'The Sacking of Balbriggan' and was widely reported as an atrocity. Though well documented, it is rarely mentioned that the 'Tan' shot was a fellow Irishman. Burke had been awarded the Constabulary Medal for Gallantry for his defence of an isolated RIC hut in Moyona, County Clare. The inscription reads as follows:

> O Jesus Have Mercy on The Soul of My Dear Brother Peter Burke DI RIC of Boyounagh, Who Died September 20th 1920, Aged 33 Years And On The Soul Of My Dear Mother Winifred Burke who Died Jan 12th 1923 aged 80 Years. Erected by Mrs Eleanor Burke to their Fond Memory.

Another RIC man from the area worth mentioning is Sergeant William Leech (65034) from Williamstown. He had served twelve years in the RIC and was stationed in Limerick where he was suspected by Republicans there of involvement in a murder, for which there was little hard evidence. He was shot dead on Brunswick Street in Dublin on 8 May 1922, although the Truce had been declared on 11 July the previous year, meaning hostilities were supposed to have ended. He is believed to be buried in Kilcronan Cemetery, Williamstown.

CLONBERN

The unassuming village of Clonbern has an old graveyard worth visiting. It contains a cast-iron circular mausoleum, unique in both Britain and Ireland and modelled on the Choragic monument of Lysicrates in Athens. It was erected for Colonel Maurice Dennis of Bermingham House (1805–63) near Tuam, who died in Dalkey,

The Dennis mausoleum.

County Dublin and who stipulated that he was to be buried at his nephew's home at Clonbern. He had spent his life in the army but struggled financially and barely managed to buy his commission. He served initially in West Africa and later in India. He retired from India aged 52 and married 20-year-old Elizabeth Jane Eyre of Eyrecourt, and the couple went to live at Bermingham House. His brother John Dennis, who died in 1869 and was a noted member of the Galway Blazers, was also buried inside. The roof supports a cylindrical pedestal on which stands a funereal urn.

The mausoleum was recently restored following vandalism. The drape on the urn symbolises the separation between life and death. It is 13 feet high and 6½ feet wide. The lettering on the panels was also cast iron but has been vandalised. The curved cast-iron door moved on rollers. Inside, the lead coffins were placed on cast-iron trestles. It is well preserved because cast iron is durable and corrosion-resistant. It was designed to stand out, was originally painted white and was visible from Clonbern house, which was demolished in the 1960s. The door carries the partially missing inscription: 'Sacred to the memory of Col. Maurice Griffin Dennis, 1st battalion/60th Kings Royal Rifles who fell asleep in Jesus. This mausoleum is … Elizabeth Dennis … otherwise Eyre'.

It was recently restored by Galway County Council Conservation Office, the Heritage Council, the Clonbern Community Development Council and the Follies Trust.

Another member of the family worth noting was Lady Mollie Cusack-Smith, the daughter of Charles Trench O'Rorke (1865–1936), who was born in Dublin in 1906. The O'Rorkes and the Dennis family were linked by marriage since 1826. In 1939, she became the first female master of the Galway Blazers, a role she kept for nearly forty years, and was described as one of the most colourful characters in the hunting scene and as an embodiment of the works of Sommerville and Ross. She died in 1998. Following her requiem mass in Tuam Cathedral she was cremated in Glasnevin, and in accordance with her final wishes her ashes were spread over Bermingham House.

Another grave worth mentioning in the same graveyard is the vault of the Browne family of Fort Browne. The vault is surrounded by cast-iron railings, which refuse to decay and are adorned with

Above: The Egan mausoleum.
Right: An inscription on the Egan mausoleum.

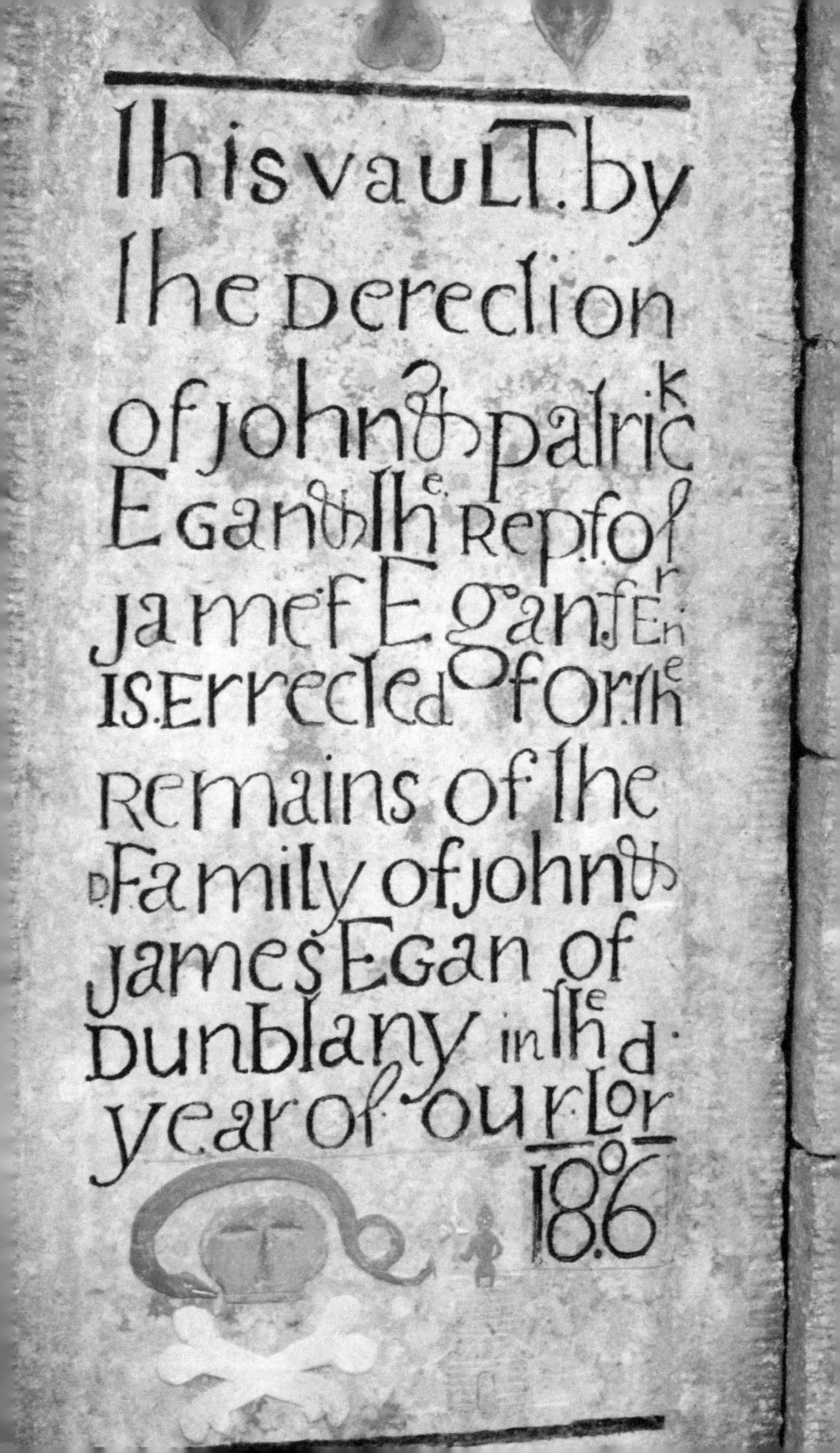

This vauLT. by
The Derection
of John & Patrick
EGan & The Rep.t of
James Egan Senr.
IS. Errected for The
Remains of The
D. Family of John &
James Egan of
Dunblany in The
year of our Lord
1806

eagles, a symbol from the family crest, and the names of family members who died between 1840 and 1915 hang on shields attached to the railings. Their house is still standing, albeit in a derelict state.

The burial vault for the Egan family bares the date of 1806. It has unusual symbols such as a snake. The figure depicted is that of a galloglass which features on an Egan coat of arms in Tipperary. The Egans have long associations with the area and were once Brehon lawyers to local chieftains. Even so, little seems to be known about which Egans are buried there and how old the burial vault is.

Also buried here is Thomas Mullen of Killavohr, who was shot by the RIC in March 1921. They had been looking for his brother who was in the IRA and took him instead. He was shot while 'trying to escape'. A memorial on the Clonbern Road marks the spot where he died. The location of the grave of Thomas Hannon, shot by the IRA on 27 April 1920, is not known, though it is known that his body was found near the village of Kigalla. He was accused of giving information to the enemy. It is easy to find graves and plaques to victims of the British military, less so for victims of the IRA.

The Brownes of Fortbrowne.

8

East Galway

Brón ar an mbás, 'sé dhubh mo chroíse
D'fhuadaigh mo ghrá is d'fhág mé clóite,
Gan chara, gan chompánach faoi dhíon mo thíse
Ach an léan seo im lár, is mé ag caoineadh!

Grief on the death, it has blackened my heart:
It has snatched my love and left me desolate,
Without friend or companion under the roof of my house
But this sorrow in the midst of me, and I keening.

PATRICK PEARSE, *'BEAN SLÉIBHE AG CAOINEADH A MAC'*
(A WOMAN OF THE MOUNTAIN KEENS HER SON)

ATHENRY

Is beag an rud is buaine *ná an duine.*	The smallest of things outlives a human.

SEANFHOCAL/PROVERB

The heritage town of Athenry was founded by Meiler De Bermingham in the thirteenth century when he bought a site there and invited in the Dominicans in 1241. De Bermingham died in Cashel in 1252 and as a benefactor of the abbey, his remains were interred there close to the high altar. His grave stone, a long narrow, recumbent house shaped slab is the only one of its kind in the county was rediscovered in the 1970s. Many of the tombs in Athenry were destroyed by Cromwellian soldiers who plundered and pillaged the town in the 1650s. The friary has two large tombs, one to the Burkes, who were raised to peerage in 1543 and the other to Lady Mathilda Birmingham, fourth daughter of Thomas, Earl of Louth, Baron of Athenry and premier baron of Ireland who died on 31 May 1788. The tomb displays fine stucco-work, a plaster applied to stone for decorative purposes, from Coade of London, dated 1790. Unfortunately much of this has been vandalized. On top of the tomb is an urn with her face depicted on it. Beside the Burke tomb is a memorial plaque to Sir John Burke who died in 1666 and whose wife Lady Mary Burke, Baroness of Athenry had the plaque erected.

The friary is locked but a key can be obtained by ringing the number on the sign and the caretaker lives close by.

In the nearby heritage centre, formerly a Church of Ireland place of worship, just off the main square is the grave of the Shaw-Taylors. Land agents had been targeted during the Land War of the late nineteenth century and this continued during the War of Independence. Frank M. Shaw-Taylor (1869-1920) of Moor Park, Athenry, was shot dead on 3 March near Coshla while on his way to the fair in Galway. He had apparently refused to divide the land among the people as the IRA had dictated. He was being driven in his motorcar when he saw a cart blocking the road. His chauffeur, James Barrett, got out to remove it and as he did so a volley of shots rang out, killing

The grave slab of Meiler De Bermingham, founder of Athenry and unique in the county.

The forgotten grave of Frank Shaw-Taylor, Athenry.

Shaw-Taylor. Barret's life was spared. The inscription on the gravestone is no longer legible to the naked eye. Also interred in the plot, watched over by an angel, is his 11-year-old daughter, Vera Cecilia who died in 1914.

MONIVEA

Dust thou art and unto dust shalt thou return.

GENESIS 3:19

The Ffrench family having been driven from the city during the Cromwellian upheaval, settled in Monivea. Their most imposing legacy is the Ffrench mausoleum located in beautiful woodland and resembling a small castle. The mausoleum, built in Wicklow granite, was constructed to receive the remains of Robert Percy Ffrench, knight of St John of Jerusalem and a diplomat based in St Petersburg,

The Ffrench mausoleum in Monivea. To the right of it is the grave of Rosamond Ffrench.

who died in Naples in 1896. His body was embalmed in Milan and remained there until it was brought back to Monivea in 1900. It is not entirely sure who designed it, but Francis Persse, brother of Lady Gregory has been suggested. The family motto, *malo mori quam faedari* which translates as 'I would rather die before being dishonoured', can clearly be seen on the façade of the structure. The mausoleum took four years to construct and no expense was spared in its construction and materials were acquired from all over Europe. It consists of a memorial chapel and a burial vault underneath. At the centre of the chapel is a fine reclining figure of Robert Percy Ffrench in Carrara marble. On the side of the effigy are the words '*Il lui sera beaucoup pardonne car il a beaucoup aime*' ('He will be forgiven much because he has loved much'). Robert Percy Ffrench married a Russian aristocrat, Sophie, the daughter of Alexander de Kindiakoff in 1863. The couple had one child, a daughter Kathleen Emily Alexandra, who was born in 1864 in Simbirsk. When her mother died, Lady Kathleen Ffrench inherited several estates on the Volga, which were later confiscated by the communists and the castles turned into museums. She led a colourful life and her biography appeared a few years ago entitled *An Irish Woman in Czarist Russia* written by Jean Lombard. She travelled extensively and travelled to her relatives in Russia. While she travelled her cousin, Rosamond Ffrench, lived at Monivea. She spent time in China as the League of Nations representative in Harbin, Manchukuo where she died in 1938. At considerable expense, her body was brought back to Monivea and buried beside her father in the crypt beneath the chapel. She left her castle and woodland to the Irish people. Astonishingly, the State demolished it and used the stone for road building. It is not clear why Rosamond, who died shortly after her cousin, is buried outside the mausoleum. Some say that a feud existed between them, while others say because she was a Catholic and her cousin was Protestant. Lady Kathleen's dying wish of leaving the woodland to the people of the area was respected but threatened when part of the woodland came under the control of Coillte who tried to sell it off in 2005 for the development of a hotel, leisure centre and nursing home. Planning permission for the development was granted by Galway County Council, but was halted by local opposition and An Taisce.

CLONFERT

Clonfert is a small village halfway between Ballinasloe and Portumna. The twelfth-century Romanesque doorway is the finest in the land, a plastercast replica of which is in the National Museum. The interior of the church has two gravestones dating back to the ninth or tenth century, inscribed with a cross and asking for a prayer

The grave of St Brendan.

for Becgan and Baclat. Some families appear to have lived in the area for several generations and I was impressed to come across a headstone from the eighteenth century in the same plot as one from the twentieth century. The dead are not forgotten in Clonfert. The cathedral is the final resting place of St Brendan, also known as Brendan the Navigator. Originally from Kerry, he established a number of monasteries along the coast, most notably at Ardfert and Annaghdown where he died in 577. He was buried here in secret to stop his remains from being stolen as relics. A simple grave slab with 'cat's paws' indentation marks, marks the spot where he is buried. Long after his death, his biography *Navigatio Sancti Brendani Abbatis* appeared which was written in Hiberno-Latin. It proved to be a medieval bestseller and was translated into several languages. The oldest known surviving copy dates from the early tenth century. The whole notion that anyone could have sailed the Atlantic in a leather boat centuries before Columbus was scoffed at until 1976, when the English explorer Tim Severin built a replica boat and sailed to Newfoundland, over the course of two years. Many things described in the *Navigatio* can be explained rationally – the Isle of Sheep for example could be the Faroes or Shetlands, the Island of Fire, a volcanic eruption around Iceland. His fame extended far beyond Ireland. St Brendan's Isle was a mythical island, supposedly situated in the North Atlantic somewhere west of Northern Africa. It was one of many mythical places on fifteenth-century maps.

Also in the graveyard is the tomb of Hubert Butler Moore, dating from 1860, who was connected to the Eyre family of Eyrecourt.

KILCONNELL

Kilconnell is situated about 13 kilometres west of Ballinasloe on the R348. The ruined friary is in the care of the OPW and is freely accessible from a path leading from the village. It was founded by the Franciscans in 1414 or 1353, depending on which source you read, by William O'Kelly, Lord of Ui Maine or Hy Many, an ancient kingdom which encompassed most of East and South Galway. Not

One of the most ornate tombs in the county, a canopy tomb at Kilconnell.

surprisingly, several O'Kellys were buried there and their coat of arms is present on some of the graves. Many of the inscriptions are still quite legible. On the Daly tomb for example the following can be made out: 'pray for the souls of Lieftenant colonel Dearmott Daly of Killimor whoe erected this monument for the use of himself and hiss brother major Teigge O Daly and there posterity 1674.'

The Bytagh tomb dates from 1685 and eleven generations of the Cloncannon family are interred here. Burials still take place within the friary and I came across a grave from 2015. It has several canopy tombs. Also interred here is local historian Martin J. Joyce who died in 1991 and was responsible for setting up the Aughrim Museum. It is believed to have had a charnel house at one stage. A charnel house or an ossuary was a building which stored human bones removed from older graves. This was necessary when they ran out of space and remains were often dug up after five years or so to make way for a new corpse. Though they existed in centuries past, few have survived. They were common on the continent and the crypt of St Stephen's Cathedral in the heart of Vienna contains rooms where the bones are piled up neatly like wood. In more modern times, the infamous mass grave on the site of the former Mother and Baby Home in Tuam may be regarded as a charnel house. A visitor to Kilconnell from 1709, Sir Thomas Molyneux, wrote of the churchyard being surrounded by skulls and bones piled very orderly, measuring 88 foot long, 4 foot high and 5 foot broad, containing about 50,000 skulls. He believed these skulls included some of the slain from the battle of Aughrim. It was also apparently a custom to expose skulls in niches of old churches. Though unfortunately he does not say where the ruined church is, the late Maurice Semple had a picture of a church window, with four human skulls lying at its base, in his book *By the Corribside*. In centuries past the skulls were even used as missiles if the site came under attack and Molyneux was horrified at this apparent lack of respect for the dead. He wrote that when Lord Clonbrock sought to bury the exposed skeletal remains he was opposed by the locals. The abbey was uninhabited by the 1780s and fell into ruin.

KILCOOLEY GRAVEYARD

From my rotting body, flowers shall grow
and I am in them and that is eternity.

EDVARD MUNCH

Located just outside the town of Ballinasloe on a hill dominating the landscape is the early Christian church of Kilcooley, which was built on the site of an earlier church dedicated to St Grellan, a contemporary of St Patrick. The grave I had come to see was that of Sergeant Thomas Craddock (56968), RIC, assassinated on the orders of Michael Collins in August of 1920. Originally from Monaghan,

Thomas Craddock, shot on the orders of Michael Collins.

Craddock had served in the Boer War and the First World War, had followed his father's footsteps by joining the RIC and had served fifteen years by the time of his death. After getting a posting to the Crime Special Department at Fry Place RIC Barracks in Athlone, he began to receive threatening letters from the IRA. He lived with his mother, a widow since 1908, and his sister. Another of her children had died in 1905. The RIC were aware that they might be ambushed and patrolled in groups of eight, but he was shot dead as he left the Great War club in Athlone on King Street. At St Peter's church, Revd T.P. Gallagher asked for prayers for the deceased's soul. The remains of Sergeant Craddock were removed from St Peter's Catholic church, Athlone, for interment here. He was given full military honours and the band of the Leicestershire Regiment led the funeral cortege. According to Thomas Costello, officer in command of the Athlone Brigade IRA, the IRA had intercepted letters by Craddock on how he would deal with the IRA. It was said that Craddock would put his revolver to the head of suspected IRA men and threaten to shoot them. Costello and two others shot Craddock as he came out of the club. Costello claimed he could have also shot the man who was with Craddock but did not as he had nothing against him.

CREAGH CEMETERY

> The cemetery is an open space among the ruins, covered in winter with violets and daisies. It might make one in love with death, to think that one should be buried in so sweet a place.
>
> PERCY BYSSHE SHELLEY, *ADONAIS*

The cemetery on the Old Dublin road is noticeable by the ruin of the eighteenth-century church. The cemetery opened in 1887. The most striking grave once you enter the graveyard is that of Thomas Harris, MP (1826-90). He was born in Athlone and spent most of his life in Ballinasloe. His grandfather was executed in 1797, which probably

Table tomb, Creagh Cemetery.

influenced his nationalist views. Matthew Harris died from stomach cancer on 13 April 1890. The monument we see today was unveiled by John Dillon in 1907. The inscription on the Matthew Harris monument reads:

> This monument was erected in memory of
> Matthew Harris ESQ M.P.
> By his fellow countrymen as a tribute to his lofty
> Patriotism his spotless integrity his unselfish devotion
> Of great powers to great public ends his lifelong services to
> The cause of Irish Nationality his sympathy with the
> Oppressed of every race and creed like the great apostle
> Preaching Christ he knew only humanity and humanity crucified
> Born 1826. Elected MP For East Galway 1885. Died April 13th 1890

Nearly half of those who answered Redmond's call in County Galway came from the town and surrounding area. Ninety-eight sons of Ballinasloe and its environs fell in conflict and not surprisingly, there are a number of First World War graves in the cemetery.

A forgotten grave of a Connaught Ranger at Creagh Cemetery.

Commonwealth graves are usually in a state of good repair, but I came one Connaught Rangers grave there which has long been forgotten and covered in lichen.

The most famous writer interred here is Eoghan Ó Tuairisc (1919–82). He was educated at Garbally College and became a primary school teacher in 1945 and served as an army officer during the Emergency. From 1962 to 1965, he edited *Feasta*, the journal of Conradh na Gaeilge. His most famous novel was *L'Attaque* (1961), written from the viewpoint of a peasant Mairtín Dubh Caomhánach, who takes part in the 1798 rebellion in Mayo. Other works include *Dé Luain*, a celebration of Easter 1916 released at a time when 1916 mania gripped the country. Both works were highly acclaimed at the time. His narrative love poem, *Dermot and Grace*, is considered his finest work. Ó Tuairisc was one of the first members of Aosdána which was set up in 1981.

WOODLAWN

Woodlawn, according to Maurice Craig is his book on Irish *Mausolea Hibernica*, is home to the largest mausoleum in the country, located about a kilometre north east of Woodlawn station, which itself was built by the Trench family in 1858 and in use until the 1970s. Though the main entrance to the estate is locked and signs warn the visitor that it is being monitored by CCTV, the demesne can be accessed by driving along a side road, known as the golden mile. As the mausoleum is on private property, I did not try to access it. The Trenchs were originally Huguenots from France and raised to peerage for their support of the abolition of the Dublin parliament in 1800. The mausoleum was built around 1790 by Frederick Trench who died in 1797. It is surrounded by a circular wall and in the middle is a circular tower which overlooks the family demesne. It continued to be used for burial until the twentieth century and Dudley Oliver Trench (1901-79) Lieutenant-Colonel and Assistant Chief Constable was buried there. In all eighteen people are buried there. The mausoleum was restored in 2001 by the present Lord Ashtown with the help of grants from the Heritage Council and Galway County Council.

GLINSK

Ballinkill Abbey in the village of Glinsk was probably built on an earlier Christian site. It contains the only effigy of a Norman knight in all of County Galway. The effigy is believed to be that of William Burke, the first Burke to come to Ireland, and dates from the sixteenth century. On a square plaque beneath it is the inscription:

Here stands
"Ye effigy of Willliam Burke
ye First Of McDavids family
who dyed in 1116 and erected by
Harry Burke 1722."

The Norman effigy at Glinsk.

The eminent historian John O'Donovan (1806-61) recorded a local tradition in 1838 that William Burke was killed in battle in France and that a French lady, who was in love with him, had the effigy made. It remained with her family for several generations until it was sent to Harry Burke who apparently bore a resemblance to the figure of the knight. Beside the effigy and set in what was once the window, is a monument to John Burke, who died in 1721.

Also in the graveyard is the navy grave of able seaman Michael Kelly who died on 14 November 1915, aged 45 and was part of the Drake battalion, a naval unit which fought on land and which saw action at Gallipoli. He appears to have died shortly before the evacuation in December of that year. He does not appear to be listed in *Forgotten Heroes* by William Henry who compiled a lengthy list of Galwegians who fell in the First World War. He does, however, appear on the Royal Navy roll of honour who lists him as dying of illness in the Haslar hospital, Hampshire.

BALLYGAR

Bíonn an *bás* mar leigheas ar an saol	Death is the cure for life.

SEANFHOCAL/PROVERB

I arrived at Ballygar to photo the plaque dedicated to Patrick Sarsfield Gilmore, late of the town and the father of the American concert band. Just outside the town, to the left at the fork in the road at the old forge, is Killeroran Graveyard. It is recognisable by its unique tower 93 foot high, a monument to local landlord Denis Kelly. The Kellys had fought for King James (a clause in the Treaty of Limerick allowed Colonel Charles O'Kelly to keep his estate at Aughrane, also known as Castlekelly) but they became Protestant in the 1740s. The Kellys ruled Ballygar and built the town when they set up a market there. Denis Kelly was MP for Roscommon and at one stage sheriff for Galway. Unlike most Anglo-Irish gentry who were not renowned for their

The Kelly memorial tower at Ballygar.

love of literature, he had a library of fifteen thousand books and had a passion for Old Irish. He was, however, known for his hatred of Catholics and used stones from a monastic ruin to renovate his castle, which would be demolished in 1919. He invested considerably in the area, financing a bridge and a courthouse.

It did not pay and by 1863 his estate was up for sale. He was married twice and had five daughters but no son. He commemorated his wives by building a round tower. There is an inscription in Irish on the tower, unusual on any monument to a landlord. The graves of his wives beside the tower, have the following inscription:

> Sacred to the memory of the two wives of D H O'Kelly. Both English women, they set themselves to the duties of their Irish house, and lived beloved by high and low and died universally lamented.

Denis Kelly was not popular, perhaps because like many landlords of the time, he controlled everything in the area and a peasant's fortune depended on his humour. A local told me that for decades after his

The Kelly mausoleum.

death it was customary to urinate on his grave whenever a burial took place. On the grave of Denis Kelly, the inscription reads:

> Denis Kelly 7 May 1877 in his 80th year. He was a Chieftain of the branch of the O'Kelly's of Screen and candidate for the Kingship of Hymany. He was an earnest Christian and a kind friend. As a tribute of respect this tablet is erected by his nephew Thomas Kelly Mahon.

Other Kellys are also buried in the graveyard. Beside an empty mausoleum is a vertical grave slab to John Kelly who died in 1813 and the inscription 'beloved and died universally lamented'.

AUGHRIM

Forget not the field where they perished –
The truest, the last of the brave;
All gone – and the bright hope they cherished
Gone with them, and quenched in their grave.

'THE LAMENTATION OF AUGHRIM', THOMAS MOORE

Aughrim has been overshadowed by the Battle of the Boyne, but in many ways it was a more significant battle, essentially announcing the death knell of the Jacobite cause. It was as significant as Gettysburg or Culloden, the difference being in the latter two cases the battlefield has been preserved, while the Aughrim site has been largely 'developed'. Seven thousand men fell and the reader may ask where their graves are? The truth is that their unmarked graves are for miles around the village and skeletal remains are being continuously uncovered. Aughrim is Ireland's largest unmarked war grave. The Irish poets referred to it as *Eachdhroim an áir* - Aughrim of the slaughter. The Jacobites were led by Charles Chalmont Marquis of St Ruth (1650 –91). He was a brilliant general but not brilliant at letting his subordinates in on his plans. The tide of battle was turning in their favour when St Ruth decided to lead the last charge himself during which he was decapitated by grapeshot. The Jacobites, now without a leader, were thrown into confusion and what should have been a victory turned into a rout. St Ruth's body was carried to the rear and privately buried during the night at the Carmelite Abbey cemetery in Loughrea. Tradition has it that five members of the Abbey community were present at the burial. The location of the grave is unknown. While the cavalry could flee to Loughrea on their horses the infantry were not as mobile. They threw away their muskets and anything that would hold up their retreat and ran for their lives. Two Irish regiments were seeking refuge in a gorge on the hillside, known locally as Gleann na Fola, the valley of blood, where, when discovered, they were given no quarter and massacred. This accounted for most of the Irish losses. The Williamite dead were buried in mass unmarked graves. The bodies of the fallen Irish were, however, left unburied and lay on the battlefield for years until eaten by wild animals. A tale is told of a greyhound whose master had been slain. The dog stayed by the body and kept the other animals at bay. He stayed there for several months until one night he saw a soldier who happened to come by that way and believing he threatened his master's bones, attacked, and was shot. There is a memorial cross near the site of Aughrim Castle as well as a small museum in the village though the landscape has changed dramatically since the construction of the motorway, which was opened in 2009 and goes straight through the battlefield site.

CRAUGHWELL

Directions: It is well signposted from the main road and a sign just before the level crossing directs the traveller coming from Galway to the right. As you go down the road the ancient cemetery is on the right in most idyllic surroundings.

In the country graveyard of Rahasane, near Craughwell, County Galway, lies the grave of a well-known Irish poet, Antoine Ó Raifteirí or Anthony Raftery. Though born near Kiltimagh in County Mayo around 1779, he spent most of his life in the Galway area. He was blind from a very early age, caused by smallpox, indeed the last thing

The grave of Raftery.

he saw was his siblings being laid out for burial. It was the custom at the time to teach the visually impaired how to play an instrument or learn poetry. Travelling poets such as Raftery taught local people their history and culture at a time when it was suppressed. Raftery himself lived through interesting times such as the 1798 rebellion, Catholic Emancipation, whiteboys, and the Tithe War. He was one of the last bards. He died in Darby Cloonan's house on Christmas Eve, 1835. According to a witness there was a sharp wind blowing at the time of Raftery's funeral but it failed to quench the candles which was taken as a divine sign. Through his poetry events important to the peasantry were immortalised that would have otherwise being forgotten. He himself would have faded into oblivion were it not for people like Lady Gregory, who had a headstone erected for him. A granite memorial was erected to him in Kiltimagh town square in 1985. The most famous poem connected to Raftery was written in New York in homage to the blind poet. Most people would have learnt it in school and it adorned the last five pound note.

Mise Raifteirí, an file, *lán dóchais is grá* *le súile gan solas,* *ciúineas gan crá.*	I am Raftery the poet full of hope and love with eyes than cannot see a silent anguish.
Dul siar ar m'aistear, *le solas mo chroí* *Fann agus tuirseach,* *go deireadh mo shlí.*	Going back on my journey with light in my heart feeble and tired to the end of my way.
Féach anois mé *m'aghaidh le bhalla,* *Ag seinm ceoil* *do phocaí folamh.*	Look at me now my back against the wall, playing music For empty pockets.

Also buried in the graveyard are the poets Patsy Callanan (1791-1865) and his brother Marcus (1789-1846), known for their laments, love songs and satirical pieces. Their graves are unmarked.

9

SOUTH GALWAY

The bitterest tears shed over graves are for words left unsaid and deeds left undone.

HARRIET BEECHER STOWE

ORANMORE

The village of Oranmore has a statue of Joe Howley (1895-1920) who was born in the village and at 18 joined the Volunteers. He commanded them in Oranmore during the Easter Rising and was subsequently imprisoned in Dartmoor Prison. He was released the following year and set about reorganising the local volunteers. When a consignment was guns went missing in December of 1920 he travelled up to Dublin to find out what happened. Little did he realise that he was being watched by an undercover RIC unit known as the Igoe Gang after its leader, Mayo man, Head Constable Eugene Igoe. He was assassinated on arrival at Broadstone railway station, the Dublin terminus of the Midland Great Western Railway and now the headquarters of Bus Éireann. When the train containing his coffin pulled into Oranmore station that evening it was met by a large number of British military and RIC. The tricolour flag was removed from the coffin and wreaths. He was buried to the rear of the old church which is now a public library. The inscription reads: 'Commandant Michael Joseph Howley/Oranmore Company/1st Galway Brigade IRA/who gave his life for Ireland at Broadstone Station Dublin 5 December 1920.'

KILCOLGAN

Directions: Take the first right turn in Kilcolgan village, go past the stables and follow the bohreen for about a mile until the church comes into sight.

Not far from Kilcolgan at Drumacoo is the St George Mausoleum, dating from 1830 and incorporated into the ruins of the mid-thirteenth-century Drumacoo church, dedicated to St Sourney. It was built to receive the body of Lady Harriet St George, daughter of the Second Earl of Howth. The St Georges, who lived in the Palladian Tyrone House, dating from 1779 and now a ruin, were apparently a model for Sommerville Ross's novel *The Big House at Inver.* They were well-known for their passion for hunting and set up the Galway Blazers in 1839 and later helped set up The Galway Races. The St Georges left Tyrone in 1905 following the death of Honoria Kane St George and sought their fortune in Dublin and America. The house was burnt down by the IRA in 1921. The plaque the entrance to the mausoleum reads as follows:

> This cemetery was erected on the site of an ancient family one by Arthur F. St George of Tyrone, Esq., in memory of the Right Honourable Lady Harriet St George, his wife, 7 August 1830. R. Fahy, Architect.

The iron doors of the mausoleum are open and it contains five stone slabs more than 8 feet in length, four of which are inscribed.

The mausoleum was restored by the Irish Georgian Society and the OPW in 1993. On the restoration plaque is the following quote from John Betjeman 'Sheepswool, straw and droppings cover, graves of spinster, rake and lover whose fantastic mausoleum sings its own seablown te Deum'.

The St George Mausoleum at Drumacoo near Kilcolgan.

The graveyard where some of the St Georges are also interred, surrounding the mausoleum is still in use and has graves that are hundreds of years old.

ARDRAHAN

Directions: To find the Bingham mausoleum follow the Athenry road from the village. It is signposted about a kilometre along the road.

The location is very isolated and locals believe the ground to be haunted. The mausoleum was erected by Sarah Selina of Cregclare House to house the remains of her husband, John Charles Robert Bingham the 4th Baron Clanmorris, who died in 1876. The mausoleum was built in 1890, several years after his death. Until then he was buried in front of where the mausoleum stands. It is set within the walls of a ruined late medieval church. His wife and brother were also buried here and all were removed in 1945 for reburial in Ardrahan Cemetery. As such, John Charles Bingham was probably the most travelled corpse in the county.

The Second World War came to Ardrahan on the 28 June 1945 when a Mosquito plane, being delivered from Canada, piloted by Flight

The Bingham Mausoleum. In the foreground, under the railings, is the spot where John Charles Bingham was first buried.

Lieutenant Gordon Frederick Ayton (51167) crashed in the vicinity of Ardrahan. As it landed it hit a stone wall and burst into flames. His co-pilot, Flight Officer Hans Raymond Anderson (J/38661) RCAF was pulled from the burning wreck by locals and survived. Ayton's remains were handed over the border and he is remembered on the Dereham War Memorial Site.

GORT

The workhouse in Gort was opened in 1841. During the famine in the mid-1840s, sheds were erected to accommodate up to 100 fever cases and a fever hospital was erected in 1848. A surviving building to the west of the workhouse site appears to comprise the northern half and what would typically have been the centrally placed entrance of the fever hospital. The fever hospital is still standing. One person of note known to have died there was Martin O'Reilly (1829–1904) a blind *uilleann* piper. Once favoured by the gentry, by the nineteenth century their status had greatly reduced and most pipers of the time were impoverished. He was born in Galway city, living at the junction of Eyre Street and Suckeen which is now St Brendan's Avenue. He had a dancehall in Suckeen before it was forcibly closed by a local priest. He took part in the Feis Ceoil of 1901 in Dublin, where he won first prize in the piper's competition. Though famous in his lifetime O'Reilly, however, ended up back in the workhouse, in Gort, where he died in 1904. A photograph was taken of him by a Father Fielding in Dublin. The communal graveyard of the workhouse is on the road from Gort to Kilbeacanty.

LOUGHREA

Nuair a thiocfas an bás ní imeoidh sé folamh seanfhocal.	When death comes it will not go away empty.

SEANFHOCAL/PROVERB

The cathedral in Loughrea was built in 1897 and to the right of the main entrance, is an imposing monument, the final resting place of Father Michael Griffin, murdered in Galway city during the War of Independence, where there is quite a trail of monuments dedicated to him. A plaque on the footpath was installed outside the house where he was taken, a stone monument at Father Griffin Road, where he

The Father Griffin tomb at Loughrea.

was shot and a well-signposted monument to the spot in the bog in Bearna at Cloghscoltia where his body was discovered.

Michael Griffin was born in Gurteen and ordained into the priesthood in 1917. He was known for his love of the Irish language and for his republican sympathies. On 14 November 1920, a man speaking Irish knocked on his door at 2 Montpellier Terrace, claiming he needed a priest. Griffin was taken to Lenaboy Castle and shot. This was in retaliation for the abduction and murder of the school teacher Patrick Joyce by the IRA. The murder caused a national and international outcry. David Lloyd George assured the House of Commons that no Crown forces were involved in Griffin's murder. An inquest held at Eglington Street Barracks declared he was murdered by 'persons unknown'. In more than 200 years the British authorities had not executed a Catholic priest, and the Auxiliaries, eager to play down their role in the murder, even lined the way of the funeral cortege. On the orders of Michael Collins a local investigation was carried out. It found that an Auxiliary named Nichols was the man responsible, but revenge was never sought. Father Griffin's requiem mass at St Joseph's church on 23 November was one of the biggest funerals the city had ever seen. Three bishops, 150 priests and in excess of 12,000 mourners, which at the time would have been more than half the population turned out to pay their respects. Every shop along the route had its shutters down and every house the curtains drawn. The city came to a standstill.

The old Protestant church on Church Street is now Loughrea's public library, though it still contains funerary memorials of a bygone era inside. The graveyard is still in the grounds and to the right of the main entrance is a grave of T.J. Smyth (7076) of the Irish Guards who fell in the First World War, aged 20. To the left of the entrance is the grave of Captain William Albert Baxby who was tragically killed on a visit to the town in 1892. Baxby was part of Baxby's circus, one of big names of the time and while promoting the circus he crashed his horse-drawn circus bandwagon into the iron railings outside Murphy's house in Barrack Street and was impaled on them. He was 30. An unusual grave just in front of it is that of Djiu Be Fu. While a Chinese community would not raise any eyebrows today, in Loughrea of the 1930s their presence was unusual. As with Baxby, he was connected to the circus and was a trapeze artist, famous for being able to perform a hundred somersaults without stopping. When the circus came to Loughrea in 1936 the 27-year-old accidently drowned in the lake. Nobody was sure which religion he belonged to and the Catholic church refused to perform any funeral rites.

Close by is also the resting place of John Oliver (8519) who took part in the Connaught Ranger's mutiny in India. He was sentenced to life imprisonment, but was released from Maidstone in 1923 at the instigation of the newly founded Free State. He was extremely bitter at being denied a military pension by the British Government and could not move on with his life. He was not to know the Irish Free State was to grant the mutineers a pension in 1935. He committed suicide in the County Home Loughrea County Galway on 18 January 1932 aged 44 which meant he was not given a Christian burial. His unmarked grave was forgotten about until the Church was being converted into the library and there were plans to demolish a nearby shed until it was pointed out that Oliver was buried underneath it. Though his grave is still unmarked in Loughrea, he is commemorated on the Connaught Rangers monument at Glasnevin.

KILTARTAN

Those who in living fill the smallest space,
in death have often left the greatest void.

W.S. LANDOR

Located in a field behind the St Attracta's Catholic church at Kiltartan Cross is the Gregory mausoleum where three members of the family are interred. The Gregorys came to Ireland at the time of Cromwell and later fought at the Siege of Derry and the Battle of the Boyne on the Williamite side. Robert Gregory (1790–1847) died of the fever while visiting his tenants during the height of the famine. His wife, Elizabeth *née* O'Hara of Raheen, was buried there in 1877 after which her son, William Gregory, born in 1817 had the mausoleum enclosed in cut stone, forming a rectangle which measures 61½ feet on the east and west sides and 72 feet on the north and south sides. William Gregory, a former governor of Ceylon, scholar and Orientalist was knighted for his services. He married Augusta Persse of Roxborough, who became Lady Gregory. He was also MP for Dublin between 1842 and 1847 and Galway in 1857. He donated several of his paintings to the National Gallery and was buried here in 1892. The burial vault was closed in 1927 and has not been used since. There is an information board with details of the mausoleum outside the museum located at Kiltartan cross. It has been recently restored and the bushes growing wild on it removed.

Not far away in the church graveyard is the grave of Ellen Quinn. She was the wife of Malachi Quinn and heavily pregnant. She was feeding her baby outside her house when she was fatally wounded by a stray bullet. The RIC had been passing by and decided to shoot randomly around them. W.B. Yeats wrote about the tragedy in his poem 'Nine hundred and Nineteen' and in lines twenty-six to twenty-eight he made reference to 'the mother murdered at her door'. Her murder

The Gregory Mausoleum.

Shot by a stray bullet – the grave of Ellen Quinn.

was defended in parliament by Sir Hamar Greenwood, the chief secretary who believed the police were right to shoot first if they thought there might be an ambush. The Ballyturin Ambush, where a pregnant woman, Mrs Blake, was shot by the IRA, may have been in revenge for this. Though she was a victim, no bitterness is recorded on the headstone, which looks quite new and were it not for the date, I would not have thought it so old.

The church ruin, dating from around the thirteenth century, has a canopied tomb. Although the tomb's façade has panels they are not decorated.

KILMACDUAGH

Not far from Gort is the seventh-century monastic settlement of Kilmacduagh, famous for its 110 foot Round Tower which is slightly slanted, Galway's very own Leaning Tower of Pisa. The site was founded by St Colman who died in 632. His tomb is a short distance west of the Cathedral and is surrounded by many large stones. There is a tradition that the soil around St Colman's grave had a healing property.

Kilmacduagh is also the final resting place of last warden of Galway, Edmund Ffrench (1775-1852) who is buried in the grave of

The lichen-covered gravestone of Pateen Donoghue, Connaught Rangers mutineer.

St Colman. This is, however, contradicted by a plaque at St Nicholas', which proclaims the last warden was James Daly, a Protestant, who died in 1864. Presumably, there were Catholic and Protestant wardens. The Ffrenchs had become Protestant by the eighteenth century but both Edmund and his brother converted to Catholicism. The Pro cathedral on the corner of Middle and Lower Abbeygate Street was built during his reign.

A lichen infested-stone reads 'In proud memory of Pateen Donoghue 1896-1941 Connaught Rangers Mutineer India 1920'. His name is also on the Glasnevin monument.

SHANAGLISH

The local graveyard at Shanaglish has a Republican plot commemorating the Loughnane brothers. Patrick, aged 29, was an active member of the IRA, while his brother, 22-year-old Harry, was active in Sinn Féin. Both were living on the family farm when, in November 1920, it was raided by auxiliaries who arrested them and took them away. They were never seen alive again. The official version was that they had escaped from captivity in Ardrahan, a story which the auxiliaries told their mother a week later. Their bodies were later found in a muddy pond near Ardrahan. They had been burnt and showed signs of torture and the letters 'IV', meaning Irish volunteers, had been engraved onto their bodies. According to the witness statement of Michael Hynes, Kinvara IRA, their hands had been tied and they were dragged behind a lorry. The mutilated corpses were photographed and the image is still disturbing. Although there was a strong British military presence in the area, they were given a full IRA funeral. Also interred in the same plot are the remains of 22-year-old Michael Kelly of Killeen, Gort, 'resting where no shadows fall'.

The graves of the Loughnane brothers.

KINVARA

I came to Kinvara to find the grave of Thomas Morris, one of Galway's unexplored 'disappeared', though I knew it would be difficult. Morris was shot by the IRA, not the British, so the likelihood of a monument to him was slim. I remember watching Professor

Eunan O'Halpin's documentary, *In the Name of the Republic*, broadcast in 2013, which focused largely on the 'disappeared' in Munster. I wondered how many people had been 'disappeared' in Galway?

Thomas Morris served fourteen years with the RIC and later, during the First World War, with the Royal Irish Fusiliers. After the war he was demobilised and went to live with his sister, about a mile from Kinvara. At 11.30 p.m. on the night of 2 April 1921 three armed and masked men came for him and shot him at Crushoa Cross. A note tied around his neck declared he was a convicted spy and had been executed by the IRA. The shooting was reported in the *Irish Independent* of 6 April 1921 and denounced by the local priest who did not believe anyone from the parish was involved. Former IRA man Michael Hynes of Dungora, mentioned the incident briefly to the Bureau of Military History in 1955 and said of Morris that he 'tramped around the country like a beggar'. No priest was allowed at the execution, lest he talk them out of it. It seems that the evidence to support his execution as an informer was flimsy, but his background; ex-RIC and ex-British military would have sufficed. I spoke to local historian John Mahony who believed Morris was an informer and mentioned a bull dog webley pocket revolver was taken off him at the time of his death, a weapon which he believed was only issued to British agents.

I went to see his grand-niece, Eileen Morris, in Kinvara who told me the matter was never discussed in the family and they were never sure exactly why he was murdered. It is not known who murdered Morris. What is known is that the Sunday after the murder, his sister went to mass and cursed four individuals and the curse came to pass. Of one she said he would never grow old enough to smoke a pipe and sure enough he died young; of another she said he would die with his stomach hanging out and he died in the operating theatre. I went to Mount Cross, Old Cemetery hoping to find a grave marker but could not find anything, though admittedly several inscriptions were weathered beyond recognition.

10

Galwegians of Note Buried Outside the County

> Graveyards are crammed with narratives, all of which end in death. Gravestones are permanent marks we leave to give notice to future generations that we were once in the world – the sign made, just as we leave, that we were here. They are laid out in neat rows, a grid to impose order on the enormous tangle of human existence.
>
> FRANCES STONOR SAUNDERS

With a population as mobile as Galway's, it comes as no surprise that so many Galwegians of note are buried outside the county. Many died tragically, such as the 650 Galwegians who fell in the First World War, which was until very recently a taboo topic. Nothing struck more fear into Galway families than the sight of an approaching telegraph boy, the unwitting bearer of tragic news. Eight illuminated volumes, containing the names of the Irish fallen were compiled in 1923 and are on display at Islandbridge in Dublin but there is no singular monument to all Galwegians who fell and whose names are too numerous to be mentioned here. William Henry wrote about them in his book *Forgotten Heroes* and Richard Abbott compiled a list of RIC casualties during the War of Independence in his book *Police Casualties in Ireland 1919-1922*.

Twenty-seven RIC casualties during the War of Independence were from Galway, some of whom I write about here. There are memorials to deceased RIC men at both Mount Jerome and Glasnevin. For those looking for information on IRA casualties I would recommend contacting the National Graves Association. The following is a list of selected men and women in alphabetical order of all backgrounds and hues, unified by their shared Galway heritage.

Nora Barnacle (1884-1951) was born at Galway City Workhouse which also served as the city's hospital. She was the inspiration for much of James Joyce's work such as the figure of Greta Conroy in *The Dead* and Molly Bloom is *Ulysses*. Her first encounter with Joyce became immortalised in the pages of *Ulysses*. They left Ireland and Joyce's father commented on their departure that like a barnacle she would cling to him and though they were engaged for nearly thirty years the couple was inseparable. Indeed, after Joyce died in Zurich in 1941 Barnacle would not leave the city for this very reason. She tried to have his body brought back to Ireland but unlike W.B .Yeats, official Ireland was not interested. She died of renal failure and was initially buried in a different part of Fluntern Cemetery, but the inseparable lovers were reunited in the same grave by the city council in 1966 and given a grave of honour. Their son Georgio is also buried there, while their daughter Lucia is interred in Kingsthorpe Cemetery.

Thomas Henry Burke (1829-82), of Waterslade House, Knocknagur, Tuam, was Permanent Under-Secretary for Ireland and as such not fondly regarded by Nationalists who referred to him as a 'Castle rat'. Along with Lord Frederick Cavendish, the Chief Secretary for Ireland, he was assassinated by a group called the Invincibles, a murder which shocked the British establishment. He was buried at Glasnevin. A very discreet stone cross in white pebbles in the Phoenix Park across from Áras an Uachtaráin marks the spot where both men were assassinated. Although I thought I knew where it was, I could only find it with the help of a park ranger. His grave at Glasnevin is located at Plot Zb 74 & 75 not very far away from the visitors' centre. There are two monuments. The obelisk has an inscription which is hard to read:

> To the memory of Thomas Henry Burke, Under Secretary to the Lord Lieutenant of Ireland. Assassinated in the Phoenix Park. This monument is erected by his many friends among the Irish Resident Magistrates as a mark of their appreciation of his high character and eminent public service. RIP.

Burke is not buried within the monument but in his father's grave adjacent to the path a few yards away. That inscription reads: 'Sacred to the memory of Thomas Henry Burke Esq. who was murdered in the Phoenix Park May 6th 1882. He pleased God and was beloved.'

Éamonn Ceannt (1881–1916) (Edward Thomas Kent) came from Ballymoe near Balinalsoe. His father was in the RIC and was transferred to Louth in 1883 and retired to Dublin. He grew up to become a skilled piper who played for the Pope in 1908. As one of signatories of the 1916 Proclamation he was executed by firing squad on 8 May after which his body, along with the other signatories, was dumped in a quick lime grave at Arbour Hill. The railway station in Galway was named after him.

Florence Conroy (1560–1629), or Flaithri Ó Maolconaire as he was known in Irish, was from Tuam (though some sources claim Roscommon). He was a Franciscan theologian and an aide to Red Hugh O'Donnell. He became Archbishop of Tuam and left Ireland with the Gaelic nobles. In 1616, under the patronage of Philip III of Spain he co-founded the College of St Anthony of Padua in Leuven. This was later to become an important hub for the production of Gaelic literature at a time when it was being suppressed in Ireland. He died in Madrid and his body was brought to St Anthony's in Leuven, where he was buried near the altar.

Cornelius Coughlan VC (1828–1915) was born in Eyrecourt. Though Galway has had several Victoria Cross winners, none of them are buried in the county and for decades they were completely ignored by historians. Coughlan was a colour sergeant with the 75th Foot, later to become the Gordon Highlanders. He fought in the Indian Mutiny of 1857 where he was awarded the Victoria Cross for his actions where he brought a severely injured comrade, Private Corbett, to safety, while under fire. Later on during the Siege of Delhi his commanding officer

Cenotaph to
Thomas Henry Burke
at Glasnevin.

was killed and he took control and encouraged his comrades forward. He later served with the Connaught Rangers and settled in Westport. He was buried with full military honours at Aughavale Cemetery near Murrisk. The grave was unmarked until Captain Donal Buckley of Military Heritage Tours had a headstone erected in 2004, which in a sign of official recognition, was unveiled by the Minister for Defence.

Sir Dominick Daly (1798-1868), of Ardfry near Oranmore, began his diplomatic career in Canada and became Governor of Prince Island before assuming the same role in predominantly Protestant South Australia. His religion initially made him a target for much criticism though he overcame this to become quite popular. He died while still in office in Adelaide. His requiem mass was held at St Francis Xavier's Cathedral and a detailed description of the funerary events are contained in local newspapers of the time, most notably The South Australian Register of 2 March 1868. As a Catholic he was buried in the Catholic section of the graveyard which caused some consternation as it was also the poor section of the graveyard. The town of Daly Waters was named after him.

Eamonn Ceannt's grave at Arbour Hill.

Count Patrick D'Arcy (27 September 1725–18 October 1779) owned Kiltullagh House. The family were Catholic and as the penal laws were enforced, in order for him to get an education, he had to be smuggled out of the country to France at the age of 14 to live with his uncle, Parisian banker Martin D'Arcy. He studied maths before embarking on a military career and served as colonel in Irish Brigade at the Battle of Rossbach in 1757. He married his cousin, Jane D'Arcy, who became a lady-in-waiting to Marie Antoinette. In 1749, D'Arcy was elected a member of the French Academy of Sciences, and had the title of count conferred upon him. He died of cholera in Paris in 1779, aged 54, and was buried in the church of St Philippe du Roule.

Eilís Dillon (1920–94) was born in Galway and lived at Dangan House and later Bearna. Her father, Thomas Dillon, was Professor of Chemistry at University College Galway. Her mother, Geraldine Plunkett, was the sister of the poet Joseph Mary Plunkett, one of the seven signatories of the 1916 Proclamation. She initially wrote children's books in Irish before moving on to write novels and detective stories. She wrote over fifty books and was translated into fourteen languages. Dillon's large historical novel about the road to Irish independence in the nineteenth and early twentieth centuries, *Across the Bitter Sea*, was published in 1973 and became an immediate bestseller. She lived in Rome and then California for several years before returning to Ireland and living in Dublin. Her writings could be described as non-militant patriotism. She is buried in Clara, County Offaly. Ray Bateson, in his book *The End an Illustrated Guide to the Graves of Irish Writers,* writes that she is buried in the Mercier family plot in St Brighid's churchyard and that neither her name nor that of her husband, Vivian Mercier are mentioned on the headstone.

John Doogan, VC (1853–1940), from Aughrim, served in the 1st King's Dragoon Guards whose commander in chief, until the outbreak of the First World War in 1914, was Austrian Emperor Franz Joseph. On 28 January 1881 at the Battle of Laing's Nek, South Africa, during a charge, Trooper Doogan saw that Major Brownlow's horse was shot from under him and Doogan, despite being wounded himself, gave the officer his and got another for himself. He was cremated at Shorncliffe Military Cemetery, Sandy Lane, Sandgate, Kent and his ashes are at Plot V, Grave 1054.

Major Richard W. Dowling (1838-67) of Knock, Milltown, near Tuam, was sent to the US in 1846 at the age of 9 after his family had been evicted. He lived in New Orleans, before settling in Heuston. With the outbreak of the American Civil War, he joined an Irish militia, the Davis Guard. With a tiny force of only forty-seven men he defended Texas against a Union invasion at the Battle of Sabine Pass. Though massively outnumbered his force held out and sank two union gunboats and took 350 Union soldiers prisoner. President Jefferson Davis compared Dowling's actions to Thermopylae where the Spartans fought the Persians. He died of yellow fever and was buried at St Vincent's Cemetery, Houston, Texas. The gravestone contains a Celtic cross in Connemara marble made by William Kelly of Tuam. A plaque was unveiled to him in 1998 and is displayed on the exterior wall of Tuam Town Hall and a book, *Dick Dowling: Galway's Hero of Confederate Texas* by Tim Collins and Ann Caraway Ivins was published in 2005.

Father Anthony Fahy (1805-71) of Loughrea was ordained a Dominican priest and was sent to Argentina in 1844 where he soon became an influential figure among the Irish and local community. He played a key role in the execution of Camila O'Gorman, a young girl of Irish descent who became pregnant by a priest, and administered the last rites to his friend Admiral William Brown, from Foxford, the founder of the Argentine Navy. He is believed to have died of a heart attack, though some accounts say he died from cholera or yellow fever. He was buried at La Recoleta Cemetery in Buenos Aires. Two streets were named after him as well as *Instituto Fahy*, a Catholic school in Moreno. He is also remembered by a plaque on the grounds of Loughrea Cathedral.

Francis Fahy (1854-1935) of Kinvara had seventeen siblings, eight of whom survived. He emigrated to England where he worked as a civil servant. He was quite active in the Irish scene and co-founded the Irish Literary Society. He is commemorated by a plaque on the gable end of his birth house, now Griffin's pub. He is buried in Putney Vale Cemetery London. His most famous song *Galway Bay*, sometimes

A plaque to Richard W. Dowling in the main square in Tuam.

referred to as 'My Own Dear Galway Bay' or 'The Old Galway Bay', predates Arthur Colohan's version, the last two verses which run:

Had I youth's blood and hopeful mood and heart of fire once more,
For all the gold the world might hold I'd never quit your shore,
I'd live content whate'er God sent with neighbours old and grey,

And lay my bones, 'neath churchyard stones, beside you,
Galway Bay.

The blessing of a poor old man be with you night and day,
The blessing of a lonely man whose heart will soon be clay;
'Tis all the Heaven I'll ask of God upon my dying day,
My soul to soar for ever more above you, Galway Bay.

St Fursa (†650), sometimes referred to as St Fursey, was a nephew of St Brendan and born in Inchiquin in the Headford area. A statue of Fursa greets the visitor at Kilursa church in Headford and lets the visitor know something of his life. It would seem that Fursa's visions of the afterlife inspired Dante's *Divine Comedy*, a fourteenth-century poem depicting the afterlife. Like many other holy men he travelled and went first to East Anglia before arriving in France. He is known to have been in Peronne, a small town near Paris, where he died. He was buried in a specially built church in Peronne. It is said his body lay unburied for thirty days while pilgrims came to view it. In this time it did not decompose and emitted a sweet odour.

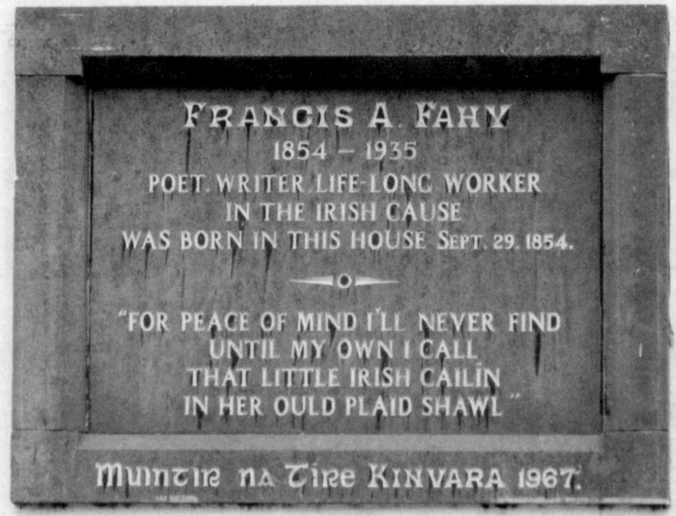

A plaque to Francis A. Fahy at Kinvara.

Private Thomas Grady VC (1835-91) of Claddagh joined the 4th Regiment of Foot (later the King's Own (Royal Lancaster) Regiment). He was awarded the VC for actions at Sebastopol during the Crimean War. His citation from the *London Gazette* of 23 June 1857 reads says he refused to retreat from his position and repelled a Russian attack. His Victoria Cross was one of sixty-two VCs personally awarded by Queen Victoria at the first investiture held in Hyde Park, London, on 26 June 1857. He migrated to Australia and was buried in Melbourne General Cemetery, Victoria. His name is also on the Australian War Memorial in Canberra. Though his Victoria Cross has survived, Grady's Distinguished Conduct Medal has not; it was ripped from his coat by a thief in Melbourne as he went to the post office to collect his pension.

Patrick Green VC (1824-89) of Ballinasloe joined the 75th Foot, later to become the Gordon Highlanders and was awarded the VC when he rescued a comrade while under fire during the Indian Mutiny. He died in Cork with the rank of colour sergeant. He is buried in Aghada Cemetery but there were several cemeteries with this name in the nineteenth century so the exact location of his grave is not known.

Major Robert Gregory (1881-1918) of Coole Park was the only son of Lady Gregory. He did not see eye to eye with his mother's close friend, William Butler Yeats whom he regarded as a parasite who sponged off his mother, while Yeats regarded Gregory as someone who wasted his artistic talents. In his poem, 'In Memory of Major Robert Gregory', Yeats wrote:

> We dreamed that a great painter had been born
> To cold Clare rock and Galway rock and thorn.

Politically, Yeats saw himself as an Irish nationalist, while Gregory supported the Empire. Gregory served in the Royal Flying Corps and was awarded the Military Cross for gallantry. He was killed in 1918 in Italy under circumstances which have never fully been explained and it may have even been a case of friendly fire. He is buried at Cimitero Maggiore in Padua, grave number A12. Despite their different viewpoints Yeats penned the now famous poem 'An Irish Airman foresees his Death':

Monument to St Fursa at Killfhursa near Headford.

I know that I shall meet my fate,
Somewhere among the clouds above;
Those that I fight I do not hate,
Those that I guard I do not love;
My country is Kiltartan Cross,
My countrymen Kiltartan's poor,
No likely end could bring them loss
Or leave them happier than before.

Nor law, nor duty bade me fight,
Nor public men, nor cheering crowds,
A lonely impulse of delight
Drove to this tumult in the clouds;
I balanced all, brought all to mind,
The years to come seemed waste of breath,
A waste of breath the years behind
In balance with this life, this death.

Patrick Griffin (1845-1925) was a Confederate soldier. It does not seem to be known where exactly where in the county he was born, only that he was from Galway and his parents were Michael and Honora. The family migrated to the US shortly after his birth and settled in Nashville, where Michael worked with the South-eastern Railroad but died in 1856, leaving young Patrick as head of the household and main breadwinner. He got a job around the age of 11 or 12 as timekeeper at South-eastern Railroad. In 1861, he left his job to enlist in the 10th Tennessee Irish regiment, a regiment about which I wrote in *Fadó Tales of Lesser Known Irish History*. He was one the youngest in the regiment and took part in all its battles. He worshipped the regimental commander Randal McGavock who was Scots-Irish and carried his body from the battlefield and buried him with the help of a Union officer also from Galway. Griffin was a battle-hardened veteran and still only 21 when the war ended. He became a successful business man in Nashville and by 1905 was the sole surviving member of the original regiment. He died on 9 June 1921 and was buried in Mount Olivet Cemetery, Nashville, close to the grave of McGavock.

King Guaire (†663), a semi-legendary king, is buried at Clonmacnoise in County Offaly. Ireland's most photographed castle, Dungaire, just outside Kinvara was named in his honour.

Colonel Patrick Kelly (1822-64) of Castlehacket, Tuam was orphaned at the age of 9 and migrated to the US where he grew up to become a merchant in Brooklyn. At the outbreak of the civil war he enlisted in the Irish 69th Infantry Regiment as a private and rose through the ranks to lead the Irish brigade at the Battle of Gettysburg. He took part and survived an ill-judged attack uphill at

Fredericksburg where the Irish fought on both sides. He fell at the Siege of Petersburg in the later stages of the war and is buried in First Calvary Cemetery in Woodside, New York.

Thomas J. Kelly (1833-1908) of Mountbellew went to America at the age of 18 and fought in the 10th Ohio Regiment of the Union army. He later returned to Ireland and joined the IRB, becoming its chief organiser. He was arrested for planning an insurrection in England. The IRB rescued him during which a constable was killed. This resulted in the execution of three men who became known as the Manchester Martyrs. He escaped to New York, where he spent the rest of his days, and was buried in Woodlawn cemetery in the Bronx, where a new headstone was erected in 2008. He is commemorated by a plaque in Mountbellew.

Brigadier-General James Lawlor Kiernan (1837-69) of Mountbellew served as a surgeon in the Union army when he enlisted in the 69th Irish regiment and fought at the first Battle of Bull Run. Kiernan was determined to join the ranks of fighting soldiers and was appointed a major in a fighting unit. In May 1863, he was wounded in the left lung, a wound he never fully recovered from, and left on the field for dead. He was captured, but soon escaped and made his back to the Union lines. He was commissioned a brigadier-general of volunteers by Lincoln but his lung injury forced him to resign in February 1864. After the war he was appointed to a consular post in Chinkiang, China, but again had to resign due to ill-health and died of congestion of the lungs. He is buried at Green-Wood Cemetery Brooklyn, plot: Section 66, plot 19229.

Sir Hudson Lowe (1769-1844) was born in Galway city, possibly Eyre Square or Middle Street, where his mother, *née* Morgan was from and where his father, John Lowe was surgeon. As an army child the family moved around a lot. He became famous as Napoleon's Jailer after the latter was exiled to St Helena, until his death in 1821. In July 1822, Dubliner Dr Barry O'Meara, who had been Napoleon's physician, published *Napoleon in Exile; or A Voice From St. Helena*. Lowe had expelled him in 1818 for trying to undermine his authority and this book was his revenge. It ruined Lowe's reputation and the British Government of the time let Lowe become the scapegoat for any perceived British ill-treatment of Napoleon. As he had spent his life travelling, Lowe had few friends to rely on, though he was supported by fellow Irish man, the Duke of Wellington. The destruction of his reputation meant that he was not awarded his proper pension and he died impoverished at Charlotte Cottage, near Sloane Street, Chelsea, of paralysis, on 10 January 1844, aged 75. He was buried without honours in the crypt at St Mark's church on North Audley Street in London. Where exactly his grave is, is not known, but he is commemorated by a plaque in the church which is no longer in religious use and not usually open to the public.

Sir Andrew Horne (1856-1924) came from Ballinasloe. After obtaining his medical degree he was elected assistant to the Master of the Rotunda Hospital. In 1885, he became a Fellow of the Royal College of Physicians of Ireland and was President of the College from 1908 to 1910.

Joyce made reference to him in *Ulysses*, as indeed he did to many contemporary people which did not always please them. He writes 'send us bright one, light one, Horhorn, quickening and womb-fruit' and refers to the Rotunda is 'the house of Horne'. Apparently, the young Joyce was in the Rotunda in 1904 and was ejected by Horne when he made derogatory remarks about the poor 'breeding like rabbits'. Horne was knighted in 1913 for his contribution to medicine. He is buried in Glasnevin.

Violet Florence Martin (1862-1915) came from Ross House, Connemara. Like many female authors of the time, she wrote under a male name, in this case, Martin Ross. Together with her cousin Edith Sommerville, the duo became known as Sommerville and Ross and produced *Some Reminiscences of an Irish R.M.* (1899), *Some Experiences of an Irish R.M.* (1899) and *Further Experiences of an Irish R.M.* (1908). The three books were set in the West of Ireland with an English magistrate as the protagonist. They were made into a hugely popular TV series in the 1980s. Martin was seriously injured in a riding accident in November 1898, from which she never fully recovered. This was a contributing factor to her death in Drishane, County Cork, in 1915. Her grave is located St Barrahane's Church of Ireland, Castlehaven in Cork.

Richard Martin (1754-1834) of Ballynahinch Castle was known as Hairtrigger Dick on account of the many duels he fought. In a falling out with a cousin he unwillingly had to face him on the duelling field and killed him, an action he deeply regretted. His second nickname, Humanity Dick, given to him by King George IV, with whom he was on close terms, was on account of his love for animals. He was a founding member of Royal Society for the Prevention of Cruelty to Animals (RSPCA), which was founded in London in 1824. He became an MP in 1776 and High Sheriff for Galway in 1782. He led a life which was anything but ordinary. He served as a colonel of the County Galway Volunteers and survived two shipwrecks. He travelled all over Europe and the Americas in the 1770s, a time of upheaval and change, and was in France when the revolution broke out in 1789. He engaged Theobald Wolfe Tone as a tutor to his family until Tone had an affair with his wife. After the election of 1826, Martin was deprived of his parliamentary seat because of a petition which accused him of illegal intimidation during the election. He had to flee into hasty exile to Boulogne, France, because he could no longer enjoy parliamentary immunity from arrest for debt. He died there peacefully in the presence of his second wife and their three daughters on 6 January 1834. The marble plaque, erected in the 1980s and written in both English and French, is as follows:

Richard Martin
1754-1834

Born in Dublin, died in Boulogne. One of the founders of the Royal Society for the Prevention of Cruelty to Animals, which held its first meeting in London in 1824. A member of the British Parliament, he piloted through the House of Commons in 1822 the first act to protect animals.

Edward Martyn (1859-1923), from Tullira Castle, Ardrahan, was a playwright and republican and became the first president of Sinn Féin from its foundation in 1905 to 1908. He introduced W.B. Yeats to Lady Gregory and together they founded the Abbey Theatre. He was buried in an unmarked pauper's grave at Glasnevin at his own request.

Caitlín Maude (1941-82) of Carna found fame as an Irish-language poet. She is best known for her role as Máire Ní Chathasaigh is the controversial Irish drama *An Triail* by Mairéad Ní Ghráda, which was staged once only in 1964 and dealt with the taboo subject of how single mothers were treated in Ireland. One of her poems, '*Géibheann*', a feminist poem about restrictions women face in society, is on the current Leaving Certificate Curriculum. She died of cancer and is buried at Bohernabreena in South County Dublin.

Jeremiah Mee (1889-1953), from Knickanes Glenamaddy, is remembered by a plaque in Glenamaddy for his role in the Listowel Mutiny. While a serving member of the RIC, he objected to the divisional commander, Colonel Smyth from Banbridge, issuing instructions which encouraged RIC men to shoot anyone suspicious looking, even those who had as much as their hands in their pockets. He told them that although innocent people would get shot, so too would IRA men and that the constables would not suffer any consequences as a result. Smyth himself was shot on sight by the IRA a while later in Cork. There was considerable support for Mee who resigned from the force along with several others and began to work with the IRA. He is buried in Glasnevin at plot WL59. His biography, *The Memoirs of Constable Jeremiah Mee RIC*, was written by J. Anthony Gaughan in 1975.

George Henry Morris (1872–1914) from Spiddal was the first commanding officer of the Irish Guards to lead a battalion into battle. He graduated from Sandhurst in 1892 and served in India and the Second Boer War. At the outbreak of hostilities in August of 1914 he took his battalion to France and was killed in action on 1 September La Forêt de Retz, during the Retreat from Mons. He is buried at Villers-Cotterêts. He was largely forgotten about until Galway City Museum held an exhibition about him in 2014/15.

Máirtín Ó Cadhain (1906-70) of An Cnocán Glas, Spidéal was a pioneer of Irish language modernism. He lost his position as school teacher at Carn Mór National School when he joined the

IRA. Between 1938 and 1944 he was imprisoned at Arbour Hill and the Curragh where he taught Irish to Brendan Behan. His most famous work, *Cré na Cille* was published in 1949 and began one of the most significant works in the language in the twentieth century. The novel, based on European folklore, centres around conversations among the dead in the graveyard. The protagonist, the cantankerous Caitríona Pháidín, dies and realises she can converse with the other corpses. Before she died she asked her son Pádraig to bury her in the 'Pound Plot', the wealthier part of the graveyard, with a limestone cross and rails around her grave. She realises to her horror her wishes have been ignored. It was never translated into English, at the author's insistence, although it was translated into Norwegian. As such and given the complexity of its Irish, it will remain inaccessible to the majority of the population though it was made into a film in 2010. Ó Cadhain was made professor of modern Irish at Trinity, which was an unusual move as he did not even have a primary degree. He became active in fighting for civil rights for Irish speakers and lamented that his beloved language could be dead before he was. He is buried in Mount Jerome Cemetery in Dublin.

Máirtín Ó Díreáin (1910-88) of Inis Mór was known for his Irish language poetry which every Irish citizen will have studied at some stage in their school career. His poetry often contrasted old and new, urban and rural. He spent most of his adult life away from his beloved Inis Mór and his heart was seemingly very much in the west, reflected in such poems as '*Faoiseamh a Gheobhadsa*' (I will find solace) It seems odd therefore that he is buried in Mount Jerome in Dublin. A plaque was erected outside the post office in Galway, where he worked for some time, and one of his well-known poems '*Fear ag lasadh lampaí*' (The Glimmerman) is inscribed on a bronze plaque on the Salthill prom.

Liam O'Flaherty (1896-1984) of Inis Mór fought with the Irish Guards on the Western Front, which influenced his novel *Return of the Brute*, an underestimated anti-war tract which dealt with the affect war had on soldiers. He returned to Ireland and dabbled in communism. He excelled as a short storywriter. In 1925, he scored immediate success with his best-selling novel *The Informer* about Gypo Nolan, who betrays his friend during War of Independence, which John Ford later turned into an Oscar-winning film. His collection of Irish stories *Dúil* was studied in schools for several years. His autobiography, *Shame the Devil*, was published in 1934. He was cremated at Glasnevin.

Patrick O'Halloran (1896-1924) lived in George's Street, Gort. Following service with the local IRA, he joined the newly formed Garda Síochána (as Garda no. 651) in 1922 and was posted initially to Dublin and then Wicklow. On 13 January 1924, Garda O'Halloran and three other guards defended themselves against a mob of fifty who attacked Balintglass Garda Station. Six day later on 29 January as Garda O'Halloran was passing the National Bank he heard sound of a struggle inside. The raiders realised they had been disturbed and left the bank with O'Halloran in pursuit. One of them fired and O'Halloran was killed immediately. Twenty-six-year-old Felix McMullen was convicted of the murder and hanged in August of that year. Unfortunately, I was unable to find the location of Patrick O'Halloran's grave.

Robert O'Hara Burke (1821-61) of St Clerans, Craughwell, served in the Austrian Army before resigning and moving to Australia where he served as an inspector in the constabulary. When an expedition traversing the Australian continent from the south to the North was announced he quickly volunteered. At the time much of the continent was *terra incognito*. The expedition was ill-prepared and Burke, who was in charge, made several mistakes, mistakes which would cost him his life. Burke and his second-in-command Wills did actually make it to the north but died on the return journey. There are places named after him such as Burke River and Burketown. Both men are buried at the Melbourne General Cemetery and Victoria Parliament had a large granite monument erected there in 1865. The inscription reads 'Comrades in a great achievement and companions in death'. A memorial cairn was also erected where their bodies were found.

Brendán Ó hEithir (1930-90) of Inis Mór was a writer and broadcaster. A nephew of Liam O'Flaherty, he studied at UCG, becoming its most famous non-graduate. His time spent there would later be reflected in his novel *Lig Sinn i gCathú* (1976), which was translated into English as *Lead us into Temptation*, one of the most successful Irish language books of the twentieth century. According to Wikipedia, he was for a time in the forties, a member of the long-forgotten radical nationalist and fascist political party, Ailtirí na hAiséirghe, which was committed to anti-Semitism, conscription, taking back the North and reintroducing the Irish language by force. Later books included *The Begrudger's Guide to Irish Politics* (1985). He married Catherine von Hildebrand in 1957 and they had five children. He died of cancer at St Vincent's Hospital in Dublin on 26 October 1990 and was cremated at Glasnevin.

Dennis J. Oliver (1823-86) of Menlo emigrated to America in 1840, living first in New York, where he became a successful merchant before moving to San Franciso in 1849 during the Goldrush with his brother-in-law John A. Glynn. Together in 1854, they purchased a tract of land on the western shores of San Francisco Bay, measuring 1,700 acres which Oliver named Menlo Park after his native village on the banks of the Corrib. A city grew from this, which in 2010 had more than 30,000 inhabitants. A plaque was unveiled to him on Menlo pier in 2013. He died of cholera in April of 1886 and his requiem mass was held at St Mary's Cathedral in San Francisco. I contacted Catherine Carlton, Mayor of Menlo Park, who put me in touch with Jym Clendenin who could tell me that he was initially buried in Calvary Cemetery, San Francisco but both he and his wife were reinterred in Holy Cross Cemetery, Colma at plot D763 4&9 in 1939.

District Inspector Tobias O'Sullivan (59193) (1877-1921) of Cloonbrone, near Cornamona, was shot dead by IRA man Con Brosnan in of January 1921 while walking with his 5-year-old son through the streets of Listowel where he was stationed. His son was not injured in the shooting and Brosnan is believed to have been haunted by what he did for many years afterwards. It is believed that he was singled out because of his ability to identify the IRA men responsible for the Killmallock attack, where O'Sullivan and his comrades repelled an IRA attack on their barracks. His requiem mass was at St James church, Dublin, after which he was buried at Glasnevin. The funeral was filmed by the British Pathé.

Where exactly **Peter Seamus O'Toole (1932-2013)** was born is unknown. He did not know for sure himself. He believed he was born in Connemara but some sources claim he was born in Leeds, where he was raised. He had two birth certificates. He had the lead role in the David Lean classic *Lawrence of Arabia* (1962). He was considered one of 1960s great hellraisers but his hellraising came to an end in the seventies when doctors diagnosed him with pancreatitis and told him his days were numbered if he did not give up the drinking. He later stared in movies such as *The Last Emperor* (1987). Although he received seven Oscar nominations he never won any, though he did win four Golden Globes, a BAFTA and an Emmy. He was eventually awarded a honorary Oscar in 2003. President Michael D. Higgins, a personal friend of his, described him as one of the 'giants of film'. He was cremated at Golders Green Crematorium in London and his ashes were, according to Wikipedia, brought to Áras an Uachtaráin. A spokesperson from the office of the President informed me that they were in the possession of his daughter.

Charles Potter (?–1921) of Dunmore emigrated to America around 1900 and joined the NYPD (6864). He drowned on 22 July of 1921 while trying to save his daughter and nephew from drowning in West Creak, Babylon, Suffolk County. He was off duty when he saw the children in difficulty. His nephew could swim to shore, but not his daughter. As he brought her ashore he stepped into a hole which he could not get out of and the water went above his head. He raised his daughter above his head and she was saved by passers by but he drowned. The circumstances of his death made him a hero and he is still remembered today. He is commemorated on the NYPD roll of honour monument at the top of panel G, located at the Empire State Plaza.

Private John Purcell VC (1814–57) of Kilcommon, Oughterard, served with the 9th Lancers and was awarded the VC for actions during the Indian Mutiny. He was killed in action a few weeks later in Dehli and was buried at Old Delhi Military Cemetery. The grave is not marked.

Michael Joseph Reynolds (1945–75) came from Cloonigney, Kilconnell, Ballinasloe. Garda Reynolds was stationed in Clontarf in Dublin when on 11 September 1975, while shopping with his family, he witnessed three armed robbers coming out of the Bank of Ireland in Killester. As they made their escape he pursued them to St Anne's Park in Raheny where he caught one of them. When he refused to release the robber his accomplice shot him. Two anarchists, Marie and Noel Murray, were convicted of his murder and though sentenced to death. Their sentence was commuted to life imprisonment when the Supreme Court ruled that Garda Reynolds had not been on duty at the time, and they were released in 1992. Garda Reynolds was posthumously awarded the Scott Gold Medal for bravery. He was buried at Glasnevin.

John Riley (1817-50?) of Clifden served in the British Army before going to America and enlisting in the American army where anti-Catholic sectarianism was rife. As a result, Riley and thousands of others deserted to the Mexicans and set up a battalion known as the San Patricios. It was the biggest mass desertion in US Army history and for decades written out of US Army history. Mexico lost the war and the San Patricos were forced to surrender. Riley was made to watch as his men were hanged. In a barbaric form of punishment, he was branded on the cheek with the letter D for deserter and flogged. He appears to have faded into obscurity thereafter. It is believed that he died in Veracruz and records for a John Riley of Clifden who died there were found a few years ago but this has been disputed by Michael Hogan, author of *The Irish Soldiers of Mexico*. The location of his grave is unknown. A small monument to the regiment was erected in Clifden. He was portrayed by Tom Berenger in the film *One Man's Hero* (1999).

Patrick Sarsfield Gilmore (1829-82) of Ballygar migrated to Boston in 1848. He is best remembered for his song 'When Johnny Comes Marching Home', a much loved American Civil War Song, like so many other son was inspired by a Irish song, in this case 'Johnny I hardly Knew Ye'. He wrote the music for 'John Browne's Body', also known as the 'Battle Hymn of the Republic'. He is recognised as the father of the American Band. He died of heart disease in St Louis and was buried in Section 10, plot 15 Calvary Cemetery, and Queens, New York.

Caomhán Seoige (1961-81) of Inis Oirr joined the Defence Forces at the age of 19 and served in the Galway's Céad Cath Irish-speaking Battalion, before serving in the Lebanon as part of the 48th battalion. Both he and Private Doherty were kidnaped from their observation post in the village of Dyar Ntar on 27 April 1981, by the Israeli-backed Christian Militia. While Doherty's body was recovered,

A plaque to Sarsfield Glimore.

Seoige's never was. A limestone monument was unveiled to him in Inis Oirr in 2015 by Minister for Defence Simon Coveney. It reads:

> Saighdiur Singil Caomhan Seoighe (Private Kevin Joyce). In memory of Kevin who gave his life for the good of world peace while he was carrying out his duties with the United Nations in South Lebanon on 27 April, 1981.

Pat Tierney (1957-96) of Galway City, an author and poet, was born to a single mother which at the time was regarded as socially unacceptable and was ostracised from birth. As a result he ended up in a series of institutions such as the infamous Christian Brothers Industrial Home in Lower Salthill. His life was series of rejections and a reflection of a cruel society. He went to America where he got AIDS. He wrote his autobiography *The Moon on my Back*. He returned to Ireland where he went to live in Ballymun and became a well-known street poet. He committed suicide under controversial circumstances-he had contacted *The Sunday Tribune* the week before and outlined his plans to kill himself. In accordance with his wishes, his interview was published after his death. He was cremated at Glasnevin and following a parade by his friends, his ashes were scattered into the Liffey.

Sir Gerard Lally (?-1737) of Tullendaly, Tuam, fought for King James and went to France in the aftermath of the Williamite War where he served as lieutenant colonel in the Dillon Regiment, which was commanded by his cousin. In 1701, while stationed at Romans-sur-Isère, he married Anne Marie de Bressac and the couple had one son, Thomas Arthur Lally, who was born in Romans in 1702. Both father and son fought in the War of Polish Succession. According to family lore, Sir Gerard heard the Tullendaly funeral bell tolling while in Arras, a sign of a death within the family. He died soon after and is buried there. Thomas Arthur went on to fight at the Battle of Fontenoy. Around 1755 he was created Count de Lally and Baron de Tollendal in the French Peerage. He fell from grace with the French while fighting in India and was beheaded in 1766 and buried in the chapel of the Blessed Virgin in church of St Jean de Grève. His son and Voltaire fought to clear his name and he was rehabilitated in 1778. The Lally family are commemorated by a cenotaph at Tullendaly, where the ancient poets once assembled and where their home once stood. It was

The Lally cenotaph at Tullendaly.

difficult to locate and it is only thanks to the staff of Tuam library that I was able to locate it and I am very much in their debt. The inscription on the monument is no longer legible but believed to have read: 'IHS pray for the soul of James Lally and his family 1673.'

General Sir Bryan Thomas Mahon KCB, KCVO, PC, DSO (1862–1930), of Belleville Athenry, Mahon served as a lieutenant in 1883 under Kitchener in the Sudan. He later fought in the Boer War where he played an important role in the relief of Mafeking. He commanded the Tenth Irish Division during the Galipoli campaign in the First World War and was given command of the British army in Ireland between 1917 and 1919. After his retirement in 1921, he was appointed a senator of the Irish Free State. He died in Dublin and was buried in Mullaboden, Ballymore Eustace.

Nine passengers from Galway are known to have travelled on the *Titanic*, which sank on the night of 14 April 1912. The rescue boats could not cope with all the corpses and many were buried at sea without ever having been properly identified, although some were identified by post-mortem photographs. The following were lost at sea and their bodies never identified:

John Flynn, Carrowhakin, Clonbur.

Martin Gallagher, Currafarry, Caltra. He is known to have helped several women into lifeboats, who would have otherwise drowned.

Andrew Keane, 20, Derrydonnell, Athenry.

Thomas Kilgannon – Currafarry, Caltra.

Patrick Shaughnessy, 24, Tynagh, Co Galway.

Thomas Smyth, Chapelfinnerty, Caltra.

Another native of Caltra, Ellie Mockler from Currafarry, survived and became a Mercy Nun in New York. She was recused with Margaret Mannion in a lifeboat which was only partially full. Mannion died in Clontuskert in 1970. Mockler died in 1984 at the age of 95 and was buried at St Joseph's Cemetery, Leicester, Massachusetts. Other women to survive the sinking included Hanora 'Nora' Healy of Athenry who died in 1919 aged 36. A monument was erected to them in Caltra. Bruce Ismay (1862–1937), president of the company which built and designed the liner and who ordered the number of lifeboats supplied to be reduced from forty-eight to sixteen, lived at Costello Lodge in Connemara for a number of years. He became a social outcast and his infamous act of cowardice, escaping with the women and children, while the men remained behind. He was known locally as '*Brú síos mé*', a play on his name, meaning 'lower me down'. He is buried in Putney Vale Cemetery, London.

Patrick Waters (1897-1920), of Loughanbeg, Spiddal was RIC constable (69079). All too often books on the War of Independence highlight victims of British violence while ignoring IRA victims. Patrick Waters became one of Galway's 'Disappeared' and until very recently the disappeared were not spoken about. At the age of 23 he had four years service and along with Constable Ernest Blight from London, was captured by the IRA in Tralee, where he was stationed. The pair were executed as a reprisal for the execution of Kevin Barry shortly after their capture, on the orders of Brigadier Paddy Cahill. According to Richard Abott they were burnt alive in a furnace. The Black and Tans assumed they were still alive and ransacked the town. What became of their bodies is not known for sure. It was also rumoured they had been shot and buried in the family crypt of the canal lock keeper William O'Sullivan. His grandson told the *Kerryman* in the mid-nineties:

> He said the two men were buried in his grandfather's family tomb in Clogherbrien graveyard, just outside Tralee. When his grandmother died in 1926, his grandfather balked at burying her in the family tomb with the two policemen, so she was buried beside the tomb. But the family of Patrick Waters were never informed.

In the aftermath of the War of Independence it still would not have been possible for the family to have made enquiries about their relative. In post-colonial Ireland the IRA answered to no one. The Irish Army's Bureau of Military History opened their files of witness statements from Old IRA men in 2003 and have since posted them on line, though some parts are still considered too sensitive for public consumption. Patrick Garvey spoke of it in 1954 to the Bureau of Military History, stating matter-of-factly that they were executed but said nothing of where they were buried. John O'Riordan also gave his statement in 1955 and says pretty much the same. The body of Waters is one of the few RIC bodies never to have been recovered. These statements were given more than thirty years after the event and as it happened during war they would not have been prosecuted so why did they not reveal the location of the bodies and why were they not pressed to do so?

Patrick J. Whelan (1840-69) was born in Galway, though the exact location is unknown. He is often referred to as a Fenian Assassin but it seems highly likely that he was innocent of the crime he was executed for, though he did know who the guilty party was. He was hanged for the murder of fellow Irishman and father of Canada, Thomas D'arcy McGee. There was little solid evidence to link him to the murder. In August 2002, his remains were exhumed from the former prison graveyard and buried alongside those of his wife's in Montreal's Côtes des Neiges Cemetery.

Thomas Whelan (1898-1921) is commemorated by an impressive Celtic cross monument in Clifden but he is not buried in his native county. He moved to Dublin at the age of 18 and joined the IRA. He was arrested in late 1920 and charged with the murder

Thomas Whelan, one of the 'forgotten ten', reinterred from Mountjoy to Glasnevin in 2001.

of Captain G.T. Baggelly, one of the British agents shot shortly before Bloody Sunday. Witnesses supported his claim that he was at mass at the time of the shooting but were not taken into account as the military court did not see Catholics as reliable witnesses. He was hanged by John Ellis along with ten other IRA men who later became know as 'the forgotten ten'. His remains, along with those of Kevin Barry, were exhumed in 2001 and buried with full military honours at Glasnevin, just inside the main gate. His name is also inscribed on a cross within the Republican plot at Glasnevin.

Alexander Young VC (1873-1916) of Clarinbridge joined the 2nd Dragoon Guards, Queen's Bay on 22 May 1890 at Renmore. He fought in the Sudan campaign and Boer War where his actions won him the Victoria Cross. He served as a lieutenant with the South African Scottish Regiment in the First World War and fell on 19 October 1916 during the Battle of the Somme. His name is included on the war memorial in St Nicholas' church, Galway and the Thiepval Memorial in France, which was erected for those whose remains could not be found.

A plaque at Claregalway Friary, date unknown.

BIBLIOGRAPHY

Websites

burkeseastgalway.com/eyre-of-eyrecourt-etc-part-i/
burkeseastgalway.com/lally/
burkeseastgalway.com/trench-part-1/
homepage.eircom.net/~oreganathenry/oreganathenry/localhistory/moniveahistoryandheritage.html
philipboucher-hayes.com/2014/06/12/tuam-new-understanding/
www.cairogang.com
www.childabusecommission.ie/rpt/pdfs/cica-vol1-08.pdf
www.csn.ul.ie/~dan/war/luftwaffeairmen.htm
www.libraryireland.com/articles/abbeyrosserrily/

Documents

The Bureau of Military History (1913-21). Witness statements from Tadhg Kennedy, Thomas Wilson, Michael Hynes, Thomas Mannion, Geraldine Dillon

Newspapers

Anon, 'The Funeral of Sir Dominick Daly' in the *South Australian Register* (2/03/1868)
Anon, 'Execution at Galway' in the *North Australian* (3/04/1885)
Cusack, Jim, 'Letterfrack: Unmarked Grave of Boy, 4, Discovered' in the *Irish Independent* (3/11/2002)
Dwyer, Ryle, 'When the Horror of War Hits Homes' in the *Irish Examiner* (25/03/13)
Gentleman, Amelia, 'The Mother Behind the Galway Children's Mass Grave Story: "I want to know who's down there"' in the *Guardian* (13/06/14)
Henry, William, 'Talking History' in the *Galway Independent* (15/05/12)

Kelly, Jim, 'A Hero in Two Nations – News of the Restoration of the Gravestone of Thomas J. Kelly' in the *Irish Examiner* (7/05/08)

Kenny, Tom, 'Executions in Galway Gaol' in the *Galway Advertiser* (3/02/11)

Kenny, Tom, 'Galway 1910-1923, The Changing Years' in the *Galway Advertiser* (10/11/2011)

Leafe, David, 'The Shameful Story of how – 200 years ago this week – a Bigoted Mob Cheated a Freed Slave out of the British Heavyweight Title' in the *Daily Mail* (14/12/10)

McDonald, Frank, 'Setback for Coillte Land Sale Plan' in *The Irish Times* (18/02/05)

McLaughlin, Brighid, 'Mannix Flynn: To Hell in Connaught' in the *Irish Independent* (22/12/2002)

Ní Fhlatharta, Bernie, 'Grave Love Affair Sees Tony Care for Forthill' in the *Galway City Tribune* (6/06/14)

O'Gorman, Ronnie, 'Unexpected Visitors during World War II' in the *Galway Advertiser* (2/04/09)

Smith, Prof James A., 'Don't let Magdalene Statue go the way of Pádraic Ó Conaire, warns Boston Professor' in the *Galway Advertiser* (5/08/10)

Journals

Bigger, Francis Joseph, 'The Franciscan Friary of Kilconnell' in *The Journal of the Galway Archaeological and Historical Society*, vol. I (Dublin, 1900), pp. 145-167

Crombie, Deirdre, 'Children's Burial Grounds in the Barony of Dunmore: A Preliminary Note' in *The Journal of the Galway Archaeological Society*, vol. 41 (Galway, 1988), pp.149-151

Knox, H.T., 'The Effigy of William Burke' in *The Journal of the Galway Archaeological and Historical Society*, vol. II (Galway, 1902), pp. 103-108

Ó Cearbhaill, Diarmuid, 'The Colahans – A Remarkable Galway Family' in *The Journal of the Galway Archaeological and Historical Society*, vol. 54 (Galway, 2002), pp 121-140

O'Dowd Peadar, 'Leachta Cuimhne or Funeray Cairns of Wormhole, Moycullen County Galway' in *Journal of the Galway Archaeological and Historical Society*, vol. 50 (1998), pp. 201-209

Stratton Ryan, Carlovian Mary, 'A Dynamic Irishman in Paris: Patrick D'Arcy, 1725-79' in *History Ireland*, Issue 2 (March/April 2010), vol. 18. Access on line at: www.historyireland.com/18th-19th-century-history/a-dynamic-irishman-in-paris-patrick-darcy-1725-79/

Tierney, Anne, *Halifax EB134 Memorial* (Tuam, 2007)

Books

Abbott, Richard, *Police Casualties in Ireland 1919-1922* (Mercier 2000)

Bateson, Ray, *The End- an illustrated Guide to the Graves of Irish Writers* (Irish Graves Publications; Kilcock, 2004)

Bateson, Ray, *Dead and Buried in Dublin An illustrated Guide to the Historic Graves of Dublin* (Irish Graves Publications; Kilcock, 2002)

Birmingham, Hubert, *Dunmore A History* (Dundalk, 2012)

Berry, James, *My Experiences as an Executioner* (London, 1892)

Blake, Tarquin, *Haunted Ireland* (The Collins Press; Cork, 2014)

Chapple, Robert M., *Cillogcillín Gravestone Inscriptions From the Graveyard of Killogilleen, Craughwell, County Galway* (The Oculus Obscura Press; Galway, 1997)

Craig, Michael and Maurice, *Mausolea Hibernica* (Liliput Press; Dublin, 1999)

Cunningham, John, *A Town Tormented by the Sea: Galway 1790-1914* (Geography Publications; Dublin, 2004)

Danaher, Kevin, *In Ireland Long Ago* (Mercier, 1964)

Dwyer, T. Ryle, *The Squad: And the Intelligence Operations of Michael Collins* (Mercier, 2005)

FÁS Galway Family History Project, *Fort Hill Graveyard* (Galway, 1992)

Feeney, Marie, *The Cleggan Bay Disaster* (Penumbra Press; Donegal, 2001)

Fleetwood Berry, Revd J., *The Story of St Nicholas Collegiate Church, Galway* (Galway, 1912; Facsimile Edition Galway, 1989)

Gaughan, Anthony J., *The Memoirs of Constable Jeremiah Mee RIC* (Mercier, 1975)

Greaney, James, *Dunmore* (Tuam, 1984)

Geissel, Hermann, *Bumps in the Fields and Crumbling Walls* (South Dublin Libraries, 2008)

Harbison, Peter, *A Thousand Years of Church Heritage in East Galway* (Ashfield Press; Dublin, 2005)

Hardiman, James, *History of the Town and County of Galway* (Galway, 1820)

Henry, William, *Galway Through Time and Tide Volume IV* (Galway Independent Newspapers, 2014)

Henry, William, *Galway Through Time and Tide Volume III* (Galway Independent Newspapers, 2013)

Henry, William, *Galway Through Time and Tide Volume II* (Galway Independent Newspapers, 2011)

Henry, William, *Famine Galway's Darkest Years* (Mercier, 2011)

Henry, William, *Blood For Blood* (Mercier, 2013)

Henry, William, *Hidden Galway – Gallows, Garrisons and Guttersnipes* (Mercier, 2011)

Henry, William, *Forgotten Heroes* (Mercier, 2007)

Higgins, Jim and Heringklee Susanne (eds), *Monuments of St Nicholas' Collegiate Church Galway* (Galway, 1992)

Higgins, Jim (ed.), *The Place of Their Resurrection – Cemeteries and Funerary Monuments Their Past and Future* (The Heritage Office Galway City Council, 2011)

Higgins, Jim, *Conamar Cathrach Fragments of a City* (Galway City Museum, year unknown)

Kelly, Cornelius, *The Grand Tour of Galway* (Cailleach Book; Cork, 2002)

Kenny, Des, *101 Irish Books you must Read* (Currach Press, 2008)

Kenny, Mary, *Germany Calling: A Personal Biography of William Joyce, 'Lord Haw-Haw'*, (New Island; Dublin, 2004)

Joyce, James, *Dubliners* (1914; this edition Penguin Classics, 2000)

Lynch, Ronan, *The Kirwans of Castlehacket, Co. Galway-History, Folklore and Mythology in an Irish Racehorsing Family* (Four Courts Press, 2006)

Lysaght, Charles, *Great Irish Lives* (Times Books, 2008)

MacCon Iomaire, Liam, *Ireland of the Proverb* (Townhouse Dublin, 1988)

Malone, Kelli Anne, *Discovering Ancient Ireland* (The History Press, 2010)

Mannion, Marie (ed.), *Memorial Inscriptions of Castlegar Graveyards* (Galway Family History Society (West), 1998)

Melvin, Patrick, *Estates and Landed Society in Galway* (De Burca, 2012)
Mercer, Derrik (editor-in-chief), *Chronicle of the 20th Century* (Dorling Kindersley; London, 1995)
Meehan, Cary, *The Traveller's Guide to Sacred Ireland* (Gothic Image Publications, 2008)
Mullally, Dr Evelyn, *Clonbern Graveyard Its Monuments and People* (The Follies Trust; Belfast, 2011)
Ó Comhraí, Cormac, *Revolution in Connacht a Photographic History 1913-23* (Mercier, 2013)
O'Donohue, John, *Echoes of Memory* (Transworld Ireland, 2009)
O'Dowd, Peadar, *A History of County Galway* (Gill and MacMillan, 2004)
Ó Domhnaill, Rónán Gearóid, *Fadó Tales of Lesser Known Irish History* (Troubador, 2013)
Ó Domhnaill, Rónán Gearóid, *Fadó Fadó More Tales of Lesser Known Irish History* (Troubador, 2015)
O'Farrell, Padraic, *The Bedside Book of The West of Ireland* (Mercier, 1981)
Ó Murchú, Daithi S., *Tuam* (Tuam, 1970)
O'Neill, T.P., *The Tribes and Other Galway Families* (Dúchas na Gaillimhe, 2013)
Ó Tuama, Seán, and Kinsella Thomas, *An Duanaire 1600-1900: Poems of the Dispossessed* (Dolmen, 1981; this edition 1994)
Phillips, Peter, *Humanity Dick The Eccentric Member for Galway* (Parapress Kent, 2003)
Prendergast, Thomas F., *Forgotten Pioneers: Irish Leaders in Early California* (Honolulu; Hawaii: University Press of The Pacific, 2001)
Robinson, Tim, *Connemara a Little Gaelic Kingdom* (Penguin, 2011)
Robinson, Tim, *Mementos of Mortality – The Cenotaphs and Funerary Cairns of Arainn* (Inishmore, County Galway, Folding Landscapes Roundstone, 1991)
Semple, Maurice, *Reflections on Lough Corrib* (O'Gorman; Galway, 1974)
Semple, Maurice, *By the Corribside* (O'Gorman; Galway, 1981)
Spellissy, Seán, *The History of Galway City and County* (The Celtic Bookshop; Limerick, 1999)
Thomson, George, *Inscribed in Rembrance – Gravemarker Lettering; Form, Function and Recording* (Wordwell, 2009)
Waddell, John, O'Conell, Korff, Anne (eds), *The Book of Aran* (Tíreolas; Kinvara, 1994)
Waldron, Jarlath, *Maamtrasna the Murders and Mystery* (De Burca Dublin, 1992; this edition 2004)
Wilde, Sir William, *Wilde's Lough Corrib* (Dublin, 1867; this edition Headford, 2002)
Welch, Robert, *Oxford Concise Companion to Irish Literature* (Oxford, 1996)
Woodham-Smith, Cecil, *The Great Hunger – Ireland 1845-1849* (Hamish Hamilton, 1962)